Praise for the Creative Real Estate Financing Series

"Chuck Sutherland was blessed somewhere along the line by being given not only a unique work ethic but a sense of how to take good ideas couple them with his own innovations, and turn them into con festations that change not only the landscape but th involved. It is important not only to dream t to turn the dream into a reality. This book is as learned over the years, coupled with techniqu and have only shared with others in his creative estate k. The tracks are now laid for those of you who read this book. He has led the way for those of you who have the desire to build your dreams and ideas on top of this foundation."

~Robert W. Steele, author of 300 Ways to Buy, Sell or Exchange Real Estate

"Chuck Sutherland has provided answers to the exact issues I have as a real estate investor, and I think most investors, new and seasoned, have: that is not only how to structure the financing, but the hands-on examples. These techniques are invaluable. Most people just give vague ideas as if their answers are top secret. Chuck has spelled it out! It makes me excited and challenged to put these techniques into practice and to continue to test and grow with them."

~Karri Speck, Real Estate Investor, Dallas, Texas

Chuck is telling you how it works in real life!!!! It has been my privilege to know and work with Chuck for many years in real estate and to attend many of the same marketing sessions. He is one of my first calls when I need help structuring a transaction and have run out of ideas. I have first-hand observed Chuck working through multi-property and multi-people transactions to find a way that each person gets the set of "benefits" they need to close by completing a transaction with people who each need different "benefits." This book is the clearest and most understandable presentation of creative financing strategies introduced I have ever read. The strategies are presented in the context of real world scenarios where the core strategy can easily be understood and applied to multiple situations. Most important, the strategies presented are strategies that Chuck and his many professional colleagues in the "people-centered" segment of real estate use day in and day out. These strategies get transactions closed where traditional financing and transactions structures totally fail. This is a book you will want to keep close to your workspace if you ever do any real estate transaction.

~James T. Wilson, SEC, EMS

CREATIVE DOWN PAYMENTS

HOW TO USE ALMOST ANYTHING AS A DOWN PAYMENT

By: Chuck Sutherland

Books By Chuck Sutherland

Creative Seller Financing (2014)

Creative Down Payments (2015)

Advanced Creative Financing (2015)

Contents

Published by Creative Real Estate Network

P.O. Box 1145, Addison, TX 75001

Info@CreativeRealEstateNetwork.com

Copyright © 2015 Charles E. Sutherland

Cover Design © 2015 Imagine! Studios™

ISBN

Library of Congress Control Number:

First Creative Real Estate Network printing, March 2015

Find Chuck Sutherland online at *http://CreativeRealEstateNetwork.com*

DISCLAIMER

This book sets forth certain general approaches and techniques concerning seller financing of real estate. Neither the author nor the publisher is a legal, tax, mortgage, or title professional. Furthermore, the author and publisher are not engaged in providing any legal, tax, mortgage, or title services. The reader is advised to seek expert assistance concerning any of these or other real estate issues.

Real estate transactions are complex—sometimes because of issues with the property and frequently because of issues with the people. Every deal is unique. Your situation (financial, personal, emotional), your needs and desires, and the needs and desires of the other parties, and the specific characteristics of the property, including state and county, require detailed understanding by real estate professionals.

The names and locations of many of the parties in these real estate transaction examples have been changed, simply out of respect for their privacy. The prices, loan amounts, exact closing costs, and loan balances have also been changed—both to protect that privacy as well as to make the structure of the examples simple and relevant. In some cases, the examples are consolidations of the specifics of several similar transactions.

Every effort has been made to make sure that all parts of this book are accurate. Nevertheless, the reader should use this book only as a general guide and not as the authority on any particular area. The author and publisher shall not have any liability or responsibility to any person or entity for the use or misuse of any material in this book.

DEDICATION

I dedicate this book to the pioneers of creative real estate techniques and what those techniques make possible for people.

ACKNOWLEDGEMENTS

I acknowledge the following past and present members of the *Society of Exchange Counselors*, who have contributed their knowledge and experience to me over the years, and those who contributed their real estate examples for use in this *Creative Real Estate Book Series*, including Chet Allen, Marilee Anderson, Steve Barker, Dana Barnes, Betty Beachum, Ed Berlinski, Bill Biddle, Corey Bishop, Ted Blank, Ron Bowden, John Brennan, Bill Broadbent, Jim Brondino, Dee Brown, Sam Brown, Larry Browning, L.R. Burton, Steve Bushey, Sandy Campagna, Rosebud Caradec, C. Charles Chatham, Rick Clark, Kim Colin, David Cook, Phil Corso, Jack Cox, Jim Crowley, Joe Crowley, Dennis Crull, Jack Dale, Madge Davis, Mark DiFranco, Wes Dingler, Chris Dischinger, Don Dobroski, Jeff Drinkard, Don DuBeau, Ernie Eden, Bob Elder, Steve England, Jon England, Nick Esterline, Steve Eustis, Jim Farley, Steve Fithian, John Fitzgerald, Peter Fortunato, Monte Froehlich, Walter Futtrup, Bob Giniecki, Leo Goseland, Hank Haden, Paul Hakim, Ebby Halliday, Arthur Hamel, Jack Harper, Daryl Hillman, Chuck Howe, Charles Huggins, Jack Hunt, Rex Jacobsma, Dick Janson, Wayne Jensen, Mark Johnson, Wayne Johnson, Will Jones, George Jonilonis, Jim Keller, Harry Kennerk, Ed Killian, Mike Lane, Tom Langel, Darrell Leason, Mark Lechner, Bill Macbeth, Paul Manza, Bill Martin, James Misco, Lance Moore, Roy Moore, Hal Morrison, Dan Murphy, Dan Murr, Marvin Naiman, Yvonne Nasch, Bryan Neal, Nick Nichols, Virgil Opfer, Tom Peterson, Hunter Quistgard, Marty Rader, Arthur Ramseur, Richard Reno, Bill Richert, Royce Ringsdorf, Ron Robinson, Danny Rosow, Alex Ruggieri, Brandon Sanders, Colby Sandlian, Richard Schindler, Jon Schweitzer, Arthur Scott, Margaret Sedenquist, Sheryl Setzen, Jim Smalley, Jim Smith, Cindy Snell, Jon Spelman, Bob Steele, Steve Steffel, Rod Stewart, Bill Stonaker, Cliff Strand, Debbie Sullivan, Don Tardy, John

Tyler, Gary Vandenberg, Ken Vidar, Lance Warner, Bill Warr, Clifford Weaver, Andy Wells, Peter West, Jim Wilson, Paul Winger, Paul Winger, Jr., Vicki Yeomans, and Bob Zink.

I also acknowledge those who have directly contributed to the editing of this second book in the *Creative Real Estate Book Series*, including my wife Marilyn Sutherland, Kristen Eckstein (and her crew), Carolyn Weiss, Karri Speck, Julia Kappel, Chris Brassard, John Godbey, and Susan Bowman.

WHO IS CHUCK SUTHERLAND?

Chuck Sutherland is a national real estate developer, consultant, and speaker. He has been engaged in the creative real estate field for more than forty years. During that time, Chuck has both worked with, and learned from, some of the most creative real estate professionals in North America to make transactions in almost any circumstance.

Chuck Sutherland's *Creative Real Estate Seminars* are in high demand among buyers, sellers, and real estate agents seeking new approaches to making real estate deals. When you work with Chuck, he brings creative ideas for potential deals and works with all players to close the real estate deal, develop properties, and turn around properties for added value.

In 2010, Chuck shared the *Society of Exchange Counselors* award for the "Most Creative Transaction of the Year." The transaction involved the exchange of fifteen different properties in five states among four different parties. In this transaction, he effectively demonstrated that a properly crafted deal with outstanding benefits for every party is almost impossible to be pulled apart by circumstances.

In this series of books on creative real estate, Chuck intends to help you gain the knowledge and ideas that you can use to make more and better real estate transactions to benefit yourself and others. If you would like to increase your knowledge of creative real estate further, check out Chuck's books and seminars at *http://ChuckSutherlandOnAmazon.com* and go to the *http://CreativeRealEstateNetwork.com*. You can also reach Chuck Sutherland by sending an email to *Chuck@CreativeRealEstate-Network.com*.

A FREE GIFT FOR READING THIS BOOK

As a token of our appreciation for your reading this book, we are offering you a free gift:

A *Free Creative Down Payment Checklist* for you to use in applying Creative Down Payments to everyday real estate transactions.

With this checklist, you will discover:

> How to determine when you might use creative seller financing strategies.
>
> How to enlist other parties in a transaction to consider creative financing.
>
> How to pick which strategy to use for different types of transaction.

Go to *http://CreativeRealEstateNetwork.com/freegift2* to sign up for the Free Creative Down Payment Checklist.

This free checklist is just one of the many benefits of the *Creative Real Estate Book Series*.

I wish you great success in your real estate future!

Chuck Sutherland

THE CREATIVE REAL ESTATE BOOK SERIES

You want to buy, sell, or finance properties. You may have many opportunities and ideas for doing real estate deals. Yet, you may be constantly battling one of the biggest issues—financing. You may also constantly be asking yourself these kinds of questions:

- Where do I find the money to do a deal and/or where do my buyers get the financing to close the deal?

- How can I help my buyers get the financing they need so they will buy my property?

Financing, or the lack of financing, seems always to be in the way of closing the deals that you want, or need, to close. "But what can I do?" you ask. "I can't control the financing market!"

Well, maybe you can, if you are in the amazing world of creative real estate financing.

That is what this book on creative seller financing and other books in the *Creative Real Estate Book Series* are about—the art and science of creatively obtaining or furnishing money or capital to buy real estate.

When traditional real estate financial fails to deliver, you can use creative real estate financing strategies to make and close your deals! You might say, "Wait, Chuck. What is traditional real estate financing and how is it different from creative real estate financing?"

TRADITIONAL REAL ESTATE FINANCING

Traditional real estate financing is simple. As a buyer, you go to a financial institution (such as a bank) and borrow part of the purchase price, invest your money (or money you borrowed from another lender) to cover whatever balance is necessary, and buy a property. As a seller, you wait for the *perfect* buyer to make the *perfect* offer. Then, in the end, you negotiate and *possibly* agree on a *less-than-perfect* contract. Sometimes, using traditional financing works to close the transaction; sometimes it does not work at all.

Numerous reference books and websites discuss traditional real estate financing. They all detail the same traditional sources of financing real estate: banks and other financial institutions and guaranteed or direct loans via FHA, VA, HUD, and SBA. Sometimes traditional financing is easily available; other times, the lenders' requirements make this kind of financing unavailable for many potential borrowers.

Many times, traditional real estate financing offers the most benefits to the buyer and the seller, but not always. Frequently, you have to get creative in order to maximize the benefits for all parties and, most importantly, close the transaction at all. How often have you tried to close a real estate deal but couldn't figure out how to make it work for all the parties—buyer, seller and lender—involved?

What Is Creative Real Estate Financing?

Creative real estate transactions have been around since the first homesteader traded chickens to the banker for a mortgage payment. For example, the original city hall for Royse City, Texas, was only built after the city agreed to build a two-story building and give the second story to the Landowner in exchange for the land.

You could say creative financing is "outside the box" of traditional real estate financing.

But that simplistic definition obscures the rich possibilities and benefits possible to those who employ creative real estate financing strategies. You can take these strategies and create a completely new way of working with real estate.

The financing strategies in this book and the other books in the *Creative Real Estate Book Series* do not constitute all of the creative real estate financing strategies that you can use in a real estate transaction, as there are literally hundreds. However, the various strategies in this series are a representative sample of what is possible. They will be a powerful guideline for inventing and discovering new creative ways to finance any transaction.

How to Get the Most from this Book

Included in this book are creative financing strategies involving houses, land, commercial properties, and investment properties as examples.

The examples are designed to demonstrate how these strategies apply to all types of real estate. If you find that the example does not relate to the type of property you are interested in, use your imagination and examine how it could apply to your interests.

You might think these strategies are only valuable in a "bad market"; however, many of these strategies can work in both good and challenging economic environments.

The material presented here goes beyond the traditional financing sources and methodologies. I present materials that typical investors never learn. If knowledge is power, the material included here will indeed provide you with a great deal of power. However, real power is power in *action*. I encourage you to "get into action" and *apply* this material to your real estate situations.

Do not finish this book with a bunch of ideas that are just that—ideas or theories. I am asking you to put yourself into the picture. Imagine you dealing with the situations given in each example. Imagine how you could handle it. Imagine using the strategy yourself—wrestling to solve real problems and finding real, workable solutions to those problems. Put yourself in all the roles of the described situations and examples. You never know. From one transaction to the next, you may find yourself as the buyer, the seller, the lender, the borrower, the broker, or even some other role.

If you put the ideas in this book into action, then, whether you read this book once or revisit it countless times, you will be gaining "practice" in solving these kinds of problems in your own life, in your own transactions. You will also make money!

FUNDAMENTAL PRINCIPLES OF CREATIVE REAL ESTATE

This chapter covers the six fundamental principles of creative real estate. You may have already read a version of this chapter in previous books and seminar materials. It is crucial that you not just understand the six fundamental principles of creative real estate but that you think from them. That is why I am repeating it here. Even if you have read it before, I invite you to read it again to remind yourself of the key cornerstones of creative real estate transactions. The most successful creative real estate dealmakers think from these. You can do that, too, but it does take practice.

PRINCIPLE #1: EMBRACE PROBLEMS AND CREATE SOLUTIONS

What do you think a problem is? The automatic thinking about a problem for most of us is that problems shouldn't happen. They are bad. They make life harder. They are barriers to having life work out.

Guess what! Problems are good! The dictionary defines a problem as "a question proposed for solution or consideration." That is it! A problem is simply a question to be resolved.

You want to be looking for problems to resolve, but not just any kind of problems.

You want to be looking for people problems. After all, it is people who have problems around real estate. A building has no problems, even if it is falling down. The building does not care. However, the owner might care; the lender might care; the neighbors might care; the tenants might care. Property problems are actually people problems.

A solution is also defined as "an answer to a problem." Now, we make the case that there are many possible answers to a problem, not just one. We assert that a solution is one of many possible answers to a problem. This book is intended to demonstrate that there are an infinite variety of strategies to solve problems and close your transactions. In many cases, you could apply several of the strategies in this book—and in the other books in this series—to close the transaction. You just have to structure the solution so it is a win for everyone.

If the definition of a successful transaction is who gets the best price, it is frequently in the context of win or lose. One party wins and the other party loses. However, if a real estate transaction is treated as a solution to a problem, then you want solutions where each party can view the transaction as a solution to his or her problem. This is what we mean by win-win transactions.

Open your own mind to possible solutions for the people problems beyond the conventional thinking. After all, this book is about creative real estate financing, not ordinary and usual real estate financing.

By the way, when you ask people what problems they are dealing with in buying or selling a property, the initial problem people describe is usually not the real problem. People who need to sell a warehouse or house for cash could want it to pay for a child's college, buy a home near family in another city, pay down debt, a tax bill, or buy a vacation home. The problem is not just that they need cash, but they are trying to resolve a problem in their life. What's the real problem? You cannot find out unless you know the principle of get all of the facts.

PRINCIPLE #2: GET ALL OF THE FACTS

What do I mean by facts? I define facts simply as "the state of things as they are." There are hundreds of different facts that may be relevant to a transaction.

Yet, when you really look at it, most of us are far less concerned with the facts than with our opinions about the facts. We want to agree or disagree with whether someone should or should not have done something. "They were wrong" or "You were robbed" or "They are so unfair in their lending policies." These are all opinions, not facts.

To solve a problem, you must start with the factual details of the situation: the property, zoning, the owner, the lenders, the neighbors, the community, building setbacks, and everything else that is pertinent. The more relevant facts that you can gather, the greater the chance you have of understanding the situation you are dealing with and creating the best win-win solution.

Getting the facts about the people issues requires asking questions, questions that allow people to talk freely about themselves and the issues with which they are dealing. Ask open-ended questions that elicit something more than a yes or no answer. In that way, you will learn far more than the question you are asking. As we noted in the prior principle of embrace problems and create solutions, you need to understand the people problems. To understand them, you must ask and listen.

When you are asking questions, let people know that your ability to come up with a winning solution for them and everyone else depends on their answers to your questions. When they understand you are asking questions to get the full picture in order to design the best possible solution, they will appreciate your interest. Use questions that others are unwilling or afraid to ask, such as: "What are your plans after you sell this property?" or "What is the current situation on your mortgage?" or "To what extent have you gone over your tax situation with your CPA?" You can ask these otherwise intrusive questions in an unobtrusive way.

But do note: Most of us are not skilled at asking questions to get at the heart of people's situations without asking leading questions or sounding judgmental. To become skilled at asking questions that reveals all of the facts, including the other party's real motivation, takes practice. I have spent years practicing asking questions in a way that people want to answer them. Furthermore, the skill is not developed by simply changing the wording of the question; it is also the manner in which you ask the question.

When you come from a commitment to help people, they can trust you and will be willing to open up to you. Think about a conversation you had with someone where you felt they were being critical of or judging you. When you know someone has your best interest at heart, they can say things to you and you listen rather than be defensive. Imagine if you could be that way with the other people in your deals.

From these questions, you gather the raw material to determine the problems to be resolved and formulate possible solutions. You have a more solid foundation from which you can support your situation, and can now work toward putting together a deal that works. Ultimately, the people you ask will appreciate that you asked these questions, because you will help them understand and achieve what they truly want.

Principles #3: Work with Motivated People

It is usually more profitable to work with a buyer or seller who *really* wants or needs to do a transaction. A motivated buyer, seller, or lender will *do* more to get the deal done than an unreasonable party who wants to win at the expense of others in the deal or someone who is unmotivated. The test of a motivated person in a deal is what will they *do*?

Be relentless (but still gentle) in discovering what people will "do" in order to uncover how best to put together a deal. Will they provide—or at least consider—seller financing? Will they accept other real estate as a down payment? Will they lease part of the property back after closing? When you present these options, make sure they understand why this might be a beneficial solution.

You will never put together a deal with someone who is not motivated to make the deal. I would rather work with someone who is broke but highly motivated than with a multimillionaire who has no motivation to really close a transaction. Cut your losses when you discover there is insufficient motivation to make a deal; redirect your efforts to people who are truly motivated to solve a problem.

PRINCIPLE #4: CREATE "NET BENEFITS" FOR EVERYONE INVOLVED

Many books on real estate assume that one party will win in a real estate transaction and the other party will lose. Operating that way usually results in one party attempting to take advantage of another party in the transaction, and one party guarding against being taken advantage. Either you take advantage of another person's misery and stress or you fear that he or she will take advantage of you.

That kind of deal can easily fall apart given that the only thing holding it together is the stress and misery of the other party.

But there is another way. That way is have everyone in the deal win. Create transactions where the buyer and seller can be of service to one another. However naïve you might at first think it sounds, there is a way where everybody wins.

Now, everybody wins does not mean that everybody will be completely thrilled or enthusiastic about the transaction that they are making. You are not looking to make the other parties happy in a transaction. Making people happy is a futile pursuit. But it is in your best interest to have others be satisfied with the transaction. People will do a transaction because of the net benefits that they receive in the transaction.

A benefit could be defined as "an advantage or profit gained from something," and a detriment could be defined as "a disadvantage or loss from something." Only if all of the perceived benefits for each party are greater than the perceived detriments for each party will a transaction actually be consummated. Detriments, like benefits, are completely individual to each party. What looks like a detriment to one party may be a non-issue or even a benefit for another party.

Net benefits can be *constructed* so there is enough to go around for everybody (I win/you win). In the end, there have to be more benefits/positives than detriments/negatives, or the deal will not close. The discussion about asking questions is critical to creating benefits that will be attractive to the parties involved in the transaction.

By the end of this book, you will see that an easier way, a better way, is creating transactions where there are sufficient net benefits for everybody. Those net benefits—the perceived benefits that outweigh any detriments—are the reason why people will complete a transaction.

Those net benefits are also the reason that others in the transaction will work with you in the future.

Principle #5: It's About The People, Not Just The Property

To do creative deal making, you must create a relationship with the other players. If you are a buyer, you must create a relationship with the seller.

If you are the seller, you must create a relationship with the buyer. It takes courage for people to think outside the box. If they do not feel that you care about them at all, they will be unwilling to think and act outside the box, and nothing will change. Relationship is the foundation—without it, you cannot build a deal that will work.

Principle #6: Employ Qualified Professionals

By employing professionals, you not only protect yourself from mistakes, but you also gain the confidence to take action where you might otherwise hesitate or freeze. In *any* real estate transaction, there are hundreds of potential pitfalls. Legal agreements, valuation issues, closing problems, property condition, ownership disagreements—any of these present opportunities for serious mistakes.

This book—or any book—cannot begin to address all of these issues. Working with competent professionals will reduce the potential for creating new problems and will reduce the impact of problems that do arise. Hindsight is always better than foresight. What sometimes looks like the best decision at the time is flawed in retrospect. You want professionals to be on your team to help guide you.

While there are many different professionals that can protect you in a real estate transaction, the most critical professionals to work with are those who work on the legal, tax, title, and brokerage issues.

Legal experts: First, be sure to obtain qualified legal counsel in any real estate or financing transaction. Remember that not all attorneys are created equal. Find a knowledgeable real estate attorney who will represent your legal interests and keep you out of trouble without making your business decisions for you. Also, make sure you choose an attorney who matches your style and with whom you can effectively work. For example, these creative real estate transactions are not traditional, so an attorney who only thinks inside the box may have difficulty with some or all of these transactions. These strategies are legal, but they are uncommon, so you need to work with someone who can think outside the box of traditional transactions. And sometimes a strategy works in one state but not exactly the same in another, so you need an attorney who understands federal and state real estate law.

Tax experts: There are also complex tax implications in any real estate transaction. Creative real estate transactions are no different from traditional transactions. Get a qualified CPA to advise you on the tax implications of any real estate transaction you are contemplating. For example, a seemingly innocent action can create a taxable event costing you thousands or more. And, like attorneys, CPAs come in all flavors. Find one who you can work with and who will advise you well. Use them in every necessary situation.

Title experts: Title companies are critical to the success of any transaction, particularly for closing services. In some states, attorneys fill this role. In other states, real estate brokers can close transactions. Regardless, you want to find a closing agent that you can count on for both responsiveness and open-mindedness. The open-mindedness is critical as you negotiate real estate and financing strategies that are outside the box. Select a title company or closing agent who has experience closing complex transactions. Work with them consistently. Train them. Be loyal.

Broker expertise: Many real estate brokers do not know or are not interested in creative approaches. Find a broker in your local area who is knowledgeable about doing creative real estate and who has high integrity. Such a professional can teach you a lot about the local market, and maybe you can teach him or her a thing or two as well. To determine if a broker is knowledgeable, use the principle of getting all the facts and especially the guidance on how to ask powerful questions. Ask the broker to explain how he or she has done creative deals outside of traditional brokering.

In summary, work with professionals who are knowledgeable and skilled, and pick the ones with whom you work best. It may take time to find the right people but it is worth it.

These are the key creative real estate principles.

STRATEGIE, NOT FULL SOLUTIONS

All of these principles are strategies to use, but they are not full solutions by themselves. You have to apply the strategy to the particular people and circumstances of the transaction. The *application* of any strategy in a particular situation can make the difference between big profits or big losses and lots of aggravation. Use good business principles in managing the details of the transaction. Get good advice.

As an example, if you acquire an option to purchase a property, but the document is flawed or it is not properly recorded, the option may be unenforceable. These kinds of issues must be included in your original contract to effectively apply any strategy.

This is why you need a professional. If you are not a seasoned investor or real estate broker or real estate tax expert, I hope by now you are clear you need to involve one or more of these experts in working with you. It is worth the extra eyes on your contract to be sure that, as part of creating net benefits, you win as well as the other party. Even if you are a seasoned investor, subtle changes in the deal could put you at risk in the deal in unexpected ways. It is best to work with qualified and experienced advisors every time.

In this book, we will not spend time dealing with the history of financing since the Napoleonic era, or the philosophical examination of the intrinsic nature of financing, or even my personal opinions about financing in the various parts of the world. This is a book about real deal creative financing techniques. It is designed to give you tools to close deals when regular financing cannot.

Our intention is to give you as much meat as possible for your discovery of these techniques for yourself.

"THE NAMES HAVE BEEN CHANGED"

I have changed the names and locations of many of the parties in these real estate transaction examples to protect people's privacy and to make the situation and the financials easier to follow. In some cases, I have also combined different people and different transactions into a single example to explain the strategy more effectively.

Throughout the book, I have capitalized various terms like *Seller*, *Buyer*, and *Investor* when they refer to a particular person or group. The purpose of capitalizing these terms is to help you track the transaction by *who* is taking action, transferring money, receiving money, etc. After all, "It's About the People" who make the transaction go together.

Whether I have disclosed their name or combined the facts of multiple transactions, I or people I personally know have employed every strategy in this book and in the entire Creative Real Estate book series.

These strategies are field-tested over many years by many different people. They work! Like everything else in life that works, however, these strategies must be used in the appropriate situation and executed in the correct manner. The strategies must also be applied within the standards of any particular state's laws and regulations.

AND NOW IT IS TIME!

Now it is time for you to explore this rich world of Creative Real Estate Financing Strategies for yourself.

Ready . . . Set . . . Go!

INTRODUCTION TO CREATIVE DOWN PAYMENTS

Conventional wisdom is that you can buy a piece of real estate *only* with a cash down payment. However, that conventional wisdom is *wrong*! You can use almost anything as a down payment to buy real estate.

I, and other people I know, have used countless items of personal and real property as a down payment on real estate. As a seller of property, I have also gladly accepted items of personal and real property as a down payment. These items as down payments were the lubricant that made a transaction possible which otherwise would not have closed.

The definition of down payment is "the part of the purchase price paid in cash up front, reducing the amount of the loan or mortgage."

This book explores the how to of a number of different strategies to use creative down payments. What could you give or accept as a down payment on real estate? Examples include:

- Real Property: Houses, Condos, Apartments, Commercial Buildings, Commercial Land, Residential Land, Recreational Land, Dock Slips

- Building Supplies: Lumber, Carpet, Plumbing, Lighting

- Financial Instruments: Stocks, Bonds, Promissory Notes, Mortgages,

- Professional Services: Legal Fees, Accounting Fees, Tax Advice, Plumbing Services, Home Improvements, Consulting Fees

- Trade Credits: Advertising Credits, Building Supply Credits,

Hotel Credits, Rent Credits, Travel Credits

- Other Personal Property: Boats, Cars, Recreational Vehicles, Artwork, Jewelry, Gemstones

- Anything else one person has that is seen as valuable and beneficial by the other party accepting the down payment

The possible variations are endless. Often, more than one type of down payment can be combined in a transaction, such as a boat, a boat trailer, a truck to pull the boat, or even a building to store the boat in during the winter.

In the remainder of this book, we explore not only *what* can be used as a down payment, but also *how* various strategies might be employed. The strategies presented do not begin to encompass the available possibilities. That will be up to you to discover for yourself in your own transactions and in working with others who have experience.

Here are the strategies we will be exploring:

- House as Down Payment

- Land as Down Payment

- Professional Services as a Down Payment

- Down Payment Equals Free and Clear Property

- Apply the Down Payment to the Monthly Debt Service

- Additional Collateral for Down Payment

- Borrow a Property as Collateral for Loan

CREATIVE DOWN PAYMENTS

- Deposit Money to Obtain a Loan

- Borrow a Certificate of Deposit to Obtain a Loan

HOUSE AS A DOWN PAYMENT

STRATEGY

A buyer can use a house as a down payment on another property. This strategy can be used whether the property is a residential property or an investment property.

A buyer can use a lower-priced house to buy a more expensive house. The seller of the more expensive house can always keep the lower-priced house as an investment. Some people even need a less expensive place to which they could move. They could even sell the lower-priced house, or they could use it as a down payment to purchase another home themselves.

A buyer can also use a house with a large equity as a down payment. The buyer can use a house with large equity as a down payment to purchase a house or as a down payment when buying an investment property.

RESIDENTIAL EXAMPLE

An Investor had located a house worth approximately $250,000. The four-bedroom, two-bathroom house, was in very good condition and was located in a neighborhood very conducive to rentals. The large university nearby had many professors and administrative personnel hungry for a decent house to rent.

The Sellers needed to sell their house because they could no longer make payments on their $165,000 loan. They were behind almost four months on their loan with $5,000 in past-due payments. The Band holding the mortgage had sent a letter stating that if the loan payments were not brought current, the bank would have no choice but to foreclose. The Sellers were desperate to avoid foreclosure, but did not want to give up their $85,000 equity (less, of course, the past due mortgage payments) to get out of their debt.

The Buyer (Investor) made a $170,000 purchase offer to buy the house by assuming the $165,000 loan and paying the $5,000 in delinquent payments. The Sellers countered, asking for $30,000 more in cash. They said that they had to have the additional cash so they could buy a smaller house with a lower mortgage payment that they could reliably make. The Seller had acceptable credit for now, but would not in the event the bank filed a foreclosure action against them.

The Investor could not see a way to buy the house at a price point that met a pre-determined yield standard. However, an application of the house as a down payment strategy made that possible.

Solution

In this case, the Investor already had a signed contract to acquire another, smaller house worth about $125,000 by taking over payments on its $95,000 loan. That Seller just needed to get out of the loan payments to move to another city for a new job. The Buyer's net cash investment in this second house was "zero" (not counting closing costs).

This second house was in the same general area as the $250,000 house, but much smaller and in poor condition. Although the Investor had the second house under contract, she was unsure whether she really wanted to complete the purchase of this smaller house, given the time and money that would be required to make it ready to sell or rent.

The Investor, however, came up with a very creative idea. She offered to buy the larger house worth $225,000 by assuming the $165,000 loan and paying the past due loan payments of $5,000. In addition, the Buyer offered to give the Sellers the equity in the smaller house that the Buyer had under contact. The other requirement was that the Sellers of the larger house also qualify for and assume the existing $95,000 loan on the smaller house.

That offer was accepted. The Buyer and her broker used three separate purchase contracts:

1. A contract to purchase the smaller house between the Investor and the Seller of that smaller house;

2. A contract to purchase the larger house between the Investor and the Sellers of that larger house;

3. A contract to purchase the smaller house between the Sellers of the larger house (now in the role of Buyers) and the Investor (now in the role of Seller).

Each of the three contracts was subject to the closing of the other contracts. In that way, none of the parties had to have the cash on hand to facilitate the next step in their purchase or sale. All the contracts closed the same day at the same Title Company with the same Closing Agent.

The Investor could have written these contracts as an exchange contract between her as the Buyer and the Seller of the larger house AND a purchase contract between her and the Sellers of the larger house. However, the Investor choose the simpler route of using three separate Purchase and sale Agreements.

Many lenders and closing agents have difficulty with understanding an exchange contract and which of the forms and procedures to follow. They do understand standard purchase and sale agreements. The use of individual purchase contracts, however, simplified the financing and closing requirements, allowing for a faster closing.

The Title Company closed all the transaction contracts together on the same day and at the same closing office. Once all parties signed all of the necessary papers, the closing agent simply distributed the necessary paperwork and funds to the appropriate parties.

SUMMARY OF TRANSACTION

Step 1: The Investor (Buyer) purchases the $125,000 smaller house from Seller #2:

The Investor (Buyer) → Takes title to the smaller house with the $95,000 loan

Seller of the smaller house → Deeds the smaller house to the Investor (Buyer)

Step 2: Investor (Buyer) purchases $250,000 house from the Sellers of that house:

Investor (Buyer) → Assumes the $165,000 loan on the larger house

Investor (Buyer) → Pays the bank $5,000 for the loan's back payments

Investor (Buyer) → Pays the Seller of the larger house an additional $30,000 (which is simply an entry on the closing statements, as we shall soon see)

Seller of the larger house →Deeds the larger house to the Investor (Buyer)

Step 3: Sale of the smaller house to the Seller of the larger house

Seller of the larger house → Assumes the $95,000 first mortgage of the smaller house

House Investor (Buyer) → Pays the Seller of the larger house an additional $30,000 (again, an entry on the closing statements)

House Investor (Buyer) of larger house → Deeds the smaller house to the Seller of the larger house

BENEFITS

Benefits to the Seller of the smaller house worth $125,000:

Seller of the smaller house is relieved of the monthly payments.

Seller of the smaller house is able to move to another city for the new job.

Benefits to the Seller of the larger house worth $250,000:

Sellers of the larger house are relieved of the high monthly loan payments.

Sellers of the larger house are relieved of the past-due loan payments.

Sellers of the larger house saved their credit in the sale by avoiding foreclosure.

Sellers of the larger house have a place to move to with lower payments that they can afford.

Benefits to the Investor (Buyer):

The Investor (Buyer) acquired a $250,000 house ($165,000 mortgage plus $5,000 in back payments), not including the closing costs of the two transactions.

The Investor (Buyer) learned a technique that she could repeat again and again. The houses do not have to be in the same neighborhood or even the same city.

The Investor (Buyer) also learned that a motivated seller will do many things that you might not normally expect. You just have to ask (in a written contract, of course).

Commercial or Investment Example

My friend Jamie, who had experience managing apartment projects, wanted to purchase an 8-unit apartment building for $240,000. The property had good cash flow with the opportunity to increase the rents over time with some minor repairs and upgrades.

The owners wanted to sell, as they had grown tired of cleaning apartments and fixing toilets. They also did not like dealing with people and were ill suited for owning rental units in the first place.

The owners of the apartment building had purchased the property to supplement their retirement income and had underestimated the amount of work it took to self-manage the apartment building. They had saved money their entire life and owned the apartment building free and clear of all loans. Furthermore, they wanted to sell and reinvest the sale proceeds in another investment to supplement their retirement income. The most important requirement was no dealing with tenants.

This was a perfect opportunity for Jamie to use his management expertise, but he had very little money. Financing was also difficult due to slow economic conditions in the immediate area.

Solution

After we brainstormed the situation, my friend remembered he had an investment partner in another apartment project who had a rental house for sale. The house had been for sale for a long time and had some issues with it. It had no curb appeal and needed a lot of painting, landscaping, and repairs to be marketable. The house was free and clear of any loans and offered for sale at $74,500. My friend asked the Investor to become a partner on acquiring the apartment building. The investor said yes!

The Investor had received an offer from a young couple to buy the house for $6,500 down and a seller-financed first mortgage of $68,000. The potential Buyers were a couple who both had well-paying jobs, but very bad credit due to health issues, unemployment, and unpaid medical bills.

After my friend and his investor inspected the apartments and reviewed the financial projections together, they offered the $74,500 house as a down payment on the $240,000 apartment building and asked the owners of the apartment building to carry back the difference of $165,500 on a seller-financed mortgage.

At first, the owners of the apartment units were interested in the offer as it did relieve them of day-to-day management responsibilities on the apartments. Furthermore, the seller-financed note did provide them with monthly income to supplement their retirement.

The owners of the apartment units decided, however, that they did not want to own a rental house. They were extremely tired of tenants and toilets. They wanted monthly income, but no tenants.

Ultimately, they did accept the offer subject to being able to sell the house. The Young Couple that was interested in buying the smaller house offered a contract to buy the house from the Apartment Sellers based upon the conditional requirement that the Apartments Sellers accept the terms on the contract they as a Buyer had previously offered. The contract for the couple to buy the house with the $6,500 cash down payment and the seller-financed first mortgage of $68,000 was accepted.

The exchange of the house for the apartment building and the sale of the house to the couple were both closed by the same closing agent on the same day. In the end, all parties got what they wanted.

By using seller financing, the apartment owners (now Sellers) were able to sell both the apartment building and the house to obtain monthly income with no hassle. The Buyers of the apartment building were able to use the Investor's equity in the house, a little cash for the closing costs, and seller financing to acquire the apartments. The Young Couple was able to acquire the house without having to qualify for a conventional loan.

SUMMARY OF TRANSACTION

Step 1: Investor exchanges the house for the apartment building:

Investor → Give Sellers of the apartment building the $74,500 house as a down payment

Investor → Give Sellers of the apartment building a first mortgage of $165,000 on the apartment building

Sellers of Apartment Building → Deed the apartment building to the Investor

Apartment Manager (Jamie) and Investor → Form a joint venture to own and operate the apartment building

Step 2: Sale of the house:

Young Couple →Give Sellers of the apartment building (now temporarily the owners of the single family house) $6,500 as a down payment on the house

Young Couple → Give Sellers of the apartment building (now temporarily the owners of the single family house) a first mortgage of $68,000 on the house

Sellers of Apartment Building (now temporarily the owners of the single family house) → Deed the house to the Young Couple

Benefits

Benefit to the Sellers of the Apartment Building:

The Sellers of the apartment building got out of the management responsibilities of the apartment units.

The Sellers of the apartment building received monthly income from both the seller-financed mortgage on the apartment building and the seller-financed mortgage on the rental house. That monthly income was much higher than they could have obtained by placing their money into a certificate of deposit at a bank.

Benefit to the Investor:

The Investor disposed of a problem rental house and acquired a passive ownership in apartments with some profit upside.

Benefits to Apartment Manager (Jamie):

The Apartment Manager (Jamie) got an ownership interest in the apartments and a monthly fee for managing the units.

The Apartment Manager (Jamie) was able to repeat the strategy to acquire more apartment units in partnership with other investors.

Benefit to Young Couple buying the house:

The Young Couple got a good house without having to qualify under their bad credit. Eventually, they repaired their credit and refinanced the loan at a lower interest rate.

KEY POINTS

The "House as a Down Payment" strategy gives a Buyer another way to acquire property without using a large amount of cash.

A house is a marketable commodity. Houses are easily financeable by traditional lenders. A house is also readily saleable at some price if there is a realistic understanding of what it takes to make the house saleable. Rather than selling the house acquired using this strategy, the new owners could also keep the house as a rental property. That makes a house an ideal down payment candidate for many buyers and sellers of real estate.

This strategy is also useful in disposing of a house that does not meet the owner's investment criteria and acquiring a property that does.

LAND AS A DOWN PAYMENT

STRATEGY

One way a seller can assist a buyer in the purchase of property is for the seller to accept land as a down payment.

Many individuals, partnerships, and corporations own land they would like to sell. Some of that land is highly marketable, with a long list of potential buyers. At any one time, one or more properties are waiting for the buyer who can put the property to the highest and best use. Conversely, other parcels of land may not have immediate uses available or immediate buyers ready to purchase.

Until a particular buyer has a particular use that warrants purchasing a particular parcel of land at a particular price acceptable to the seller, that particular parcel of land will remain unsold. However, that does not mean that the property itself is bad or permanently undesirable. Every property has its own time when development becomes most logical.

However, even if an investor has a great use for a particular parcel of land, the national, local, or even the investor's personal economic situation may prevent him or her from making the purchase. Likewise the seller, believing that the property should command a high price, may sit on the unsold property for years, waiting for a buyer to meet that price.

The truth is that all property has a current market value and a buyer at that market value. That market value may not conform to what the seller would accept or what most buyers would pay, but there is a buyer at some price and under certain terms.

All of these factors lead to an opportunity for property sellers to improve their odds of making a sale by being willing to accept land as a down payment for their real estate.

Giving an owner of land a way to use that land in a transaction can be good business for a creative seller or broker.

RESIDENTIAL EXAMPLE

I once lived in Wichita, Kansas, which is fairly close to Oklahoma, Missouri, and Arkansas. At the time I was a real estate broker and looking for new clients with whom to do business. I remembered that people who have a problem might make the best real estate clients.

One day, I realized that some of the people who owned recreational and second home lots in those three states might see their ownership of those lots as a problem. Many buyers of these lots originally intended to build a house, but later changed their plans. The lot then became more of a nuisance than a desirable asset. Furthermore, buyers originally purchased many of these lots with a small down payment followed by many years of monthly payments on the seller financing for the lot. If you have ever made these kinds of monthly payments, you know how the reason for the original purchase fades every month as the a new payments becomes due.

I further theorized that some of those people might like to use their land as a down payment on other property. To test my theory, I placed an ad in a local newspaper in Wichita that read: "Use Your Recreational Land to Buy Investment Real Estate." One of the many calls I received from the ad was from a father and son in the residential real estate business. The family owned a free and clear second home lot in Arkansas that they had purchased several years earlier as an investment. The lot was worth approximately $20,000, but there were very few buyers for vacant lots at the time in that market. There were also a large number of similar lots on the market. Furthermore, the second-home market was also almost nonexistent.

It was important to the father that the Arkansas lot be put to some productive use. They were interested in investing in single-family rental houses, but had little cash use for a down payment. However, they did have very good credit. Furthermore, they did have good knowledge of residential real estate, but did not have a clue as to how to use land as a down payment on a house.

In the process of discussing their situation and their goal to buy a house to use as a rental property, I counseled them that their land was not the same as cash. I advised them to think of their land as a medium of exchange rather than as cash. I also reminded them that there are some items that are more acceptable as a medium of exchange than other items.

For example, cash is more widely acceptable as a medium of exchange than vacant land. More owners of houses would accept cash in a transaction, but fewer would accept land. However, I told them, if they were willing to be flexible about the type of house they wanted for their rental property, we might be able to use the land as a down payment on a rental house. They agreed.

SOLUTION

I located a house for which the Seller desperately needed out of the mortgage payments. The Seller was several months behind on her payments and was in danger of losing her house and ruining her credit. The house had a real market value of $110,000 with a first mortgage of $75,000.

My client signed a real estate exchange contract to exchange the Arkansas lot as a down payment on the house and my clients would assume the Seller's debt and pay the past due payments and transfer costs of approximately $5,500. Although the total consideration was only about $100,000, the Seller accepted the contract and the lender approved my clients to assume the debt.

Summary of Transaction

Step 1: Buyer buys $110,000 house from Seller in exchange for Arkansas lot and paying past due payments

Buyers → Assume the existing $75,000 first mortgage for the house

Buyers → Pay $5,500 past due payments and the transfer costs at closing

Buyers → Deed the Arkansas lot to the Seller

Seller → Deeds the house to the Buyers

Step 2: Rent the house to a tenant

Buyers → Find a tenant, rent the house, and receive monthly cash flow

Buyers →Keep the house for the long term

Benefit to Buyers (my clients):

My clients used their equity in the Arkansas lot as a down payment on an investment house resolving their problem of having very little cash.

My clients then had a long-term investment that was building equity for them over time.

Benefit to Sellers:

The Seller received something of value for the equity she would have otherwise lost.

The Seller retained some measure of her credit.

Benefit to Lender:

The Lender obtained a credit worthy borrower who would make the payments.

The Lender also avoided having to foreclose on the property.

ANOTHER RESIDENTIAL EXAMPLE

Early in my career, I was looking to buy a house for my family. As my wife and I were raising young children, I wanted the house to be in a safe neighborhood. At the time, I had very little cash for a down payment. However, I did own twenty "paper lots" in North Dakota. A paper lot is land that someone has subdivided for individual lots, but streets and utilities have not yet been installed. Therefore, the lots are usually inexpensive.

In a brainstorming meeting with a couple of other creative real estate investors, I mentioned my desires. One of the members of the group was a local real estate broker who had a historical house for sale in a very nice neighborhood. The house was one of two houses built in the early 1900's on top of a hill in a very nice are of the city. Two brothers had built identical houses right next door to one another, even though originally there was a large amount of vacant land undeveloped around them.

Although the house could be immediately occupied, it was in need of substantial repairs to restore it to its original pristine condition. The owners had been unable to afford any of the repairs to the house that were necessary. Furthermore, the Sellers were behind on their payments to a local lender and in danger of losing the house in foreclosure.

Solution

I offered the Sellers $500 cash as the down payment plus the twenty inexpensive paper lots in North Dakota for the equity in the house. I explained that the lots were in a platted subdivision with no streets or utilities installed yet.

I also agreed to assume the first mortgage of $250,000 on the house. The Sellers countered my offer, asking me to pay the back payments of $6,000 on the first mortgage as well. I agreed to their counter offer. Because I was well known at the bank where the Sellers had their loan, we were able to close the transaction very quickly. This made both the Sellers and bank happy.

Summary of Transaction

Step 1: Close on purchase of house

Buyer (me) → Pays $500 cash as the down payment

Buyer (me) → Pays $6,000 back payments on Seller's loan

Buyer (me) → Deeds 20 paper lots in North Dakota

Buyer (me) → Assumes $250,000 first lien

Seller → Deeds house to Buyer (me)

Benefits

Benefits to Buyer (me):

I bought the house with very little cash as a down payment.

I also put the land I owned to use in the transaction.

My family loved the house and the neighborhood.

Benefits to Seller:

The Sellers salvaged some equity in the house with the lots I gave as part of the down payment.

The Sellers also kept their credit intact as they avoided foreclosure.

Commercial or Investment Example

Steve Barker of Charlotte, North Carolina, was interested in buying a hotel in Dickinson, North Dakota. Steve, a creative thinker and knowledgeable developer, had completed a great deal of real estate development in Charlotte and other parts of the United States.

The hotel was structurally in good condition but cosmetically in very poor condition. The hotel was also losing a substantial amount of money every day with no solution to the cash drain in sight. This was before the North Dakota oil boom.

Steve and I agreed to work together to purchase the hotel. He would arrange the financing of the purchase and my company would manage the day-to-day hotel turnaround and remodeling.

There were actually two separate ownership interests to acquire, one from the Landowner and one from the Hotel Operator. The Landowner owned the land upon which the hotel sat and leased the use of that land to the Hotel Operator. The Landowner also owned a parcel of vacant land adjacent to the hotel. The Hotel Operator owned the right to use the property through the long-term leasehold on the property, and owned the furniture and fixtures inside the hotel. Local lenders were not interested in making a loan on the property because of the hotel's poor condition and lackluster operating history. Furthermore, in that part of the country, lenders were not interested in making loans on the kind of leasehold interest that the Hotel Operator possessed. Instead, banks wanted a mortgage against *both* the land and the building.

Steve and I did not have sufficient cash to buy the land from the Landowner; purchase the furniture, fixtures, and leasehold interest from the

Hotel Operator; and perform the substantial remodeling required to make the hotel successful. Furthermore, because of the condition and the poor operating history of the hotel, there were no financial institutions willing to make a speculative loan in that amount.

SOLUTION

Steve and I brainstormed many different approaches to acquiring the hotel and turning it around financially. We finally arrived at a workable strategy.

We formed a new Limited Liability Corporation (LLC) and agreed to purchase the land from the Landowner for cash, contingent on our being able to purchase the hotel leasehold from the Hotel Operator. We gave the Landowner cash plus a parcel of land that Steve owned in North Carolina for the balance. That land in North Carolina was commercial land in a business subdivision adjacent to a major highway.

To acquire the hotel leasehold interest from the Hotel Operator, we offered some cash with the balance plus the land adjacent to the hotel (that we had just agreed to acquire from the Landowner). This contract with the Hotel Operator was contingent on our simultaneously closing on the purchase of the land from the Landowner.

The purchases between the LLC and the Landowner, and between the LLC and the Hotel Operator, were therefore both contingent on simultaneously closing the other purchase.

We closed both contracts on the same day. Although all the closing documents for both transactions were signed at the same time, the closings actually ended up being consecutive and not strictly simultaneous. At the closing with the Landowner, the LLC gave cash and the land in North Carolina for the entire land parcel in North Dakota, plus the vacant land adjacent to the hotel. The LLC owned that adjacent land for less than one hour as we next exchanged it with some additional cash for the hotel leasehold plus all the furniture and fixtures. That land adjacent to the hotel and the land in North Carolina were the critical elements to being able to acquire the entire property. Otherwise, there would have been insufficient cash available to make the transaction.

Because the LLC now owned both the land subject to the lease and the leasehold estate on the land, a "merger of title" was created whereby the LLC then owned the land and building comprising the entire hotel in fee simple title free and clear of all encumbrances. The LLC was now in a position to obtain financing on the hotel property for remodeling the hotel and making the hotel operations successful. However, lenders still required some significant level of remodeling and results to justify any significant financing.

My company proceeded to immediately take over operations of the hotel and begin remodeling activities. Steve's company managed the overall asset, arranged for architectural planning, and brought in design consultants to create a successful remodeling program for the hotel.

Together, Steve and I made a great team and we structured a transaction that had high net benefits for all parties. The supporting staff of the hotel and of our own respective companies contributed to the ultimate success of the hotel.

SUMMARY OF TRANSACTION

Step 1: Buyer (the LLC) purchases the land both under and adjacent to the hotel

Buyer (the LLC) → Deeds the North Carolina land to the Landowner

Buyer (the LLC) → Pays the balance in cash to the Landowner

Landowner → Deeds two parcels of land to the Buyer—the land under the hotel and the land adjacent to the hotel

Step 2: Buyer (the LLC) exchanges adjacent land and cash for the hotel building, furniture, and fixtures

Buyer (the LLC) → Deeds the adjacent parcel of vacant land to the Hotel Operator

Buyer (the LLC) → Gives cash to the Hotel Operator for the balance

Hotel Operator → Transfers the hotel building and contents to the Buyer (the LLC)

Step 3: Ownership

Buyer (the LLC) → Creates a new hotel management entity

New hotel management entity → Remodeled, operated, and turned the hotel around

Buyer (the LLC) →Received good cash flow through ownership

BENEFITS

Benefit to Buyer (the LLC):

The Buyer (the LLC) was able to stretch the cash to acquire the entire property without needing to obtain any conventional financing on the initial purchase

Together, the entire team was able to transform the hotel property and the hotel operations to be successful.

Over time, the hotel became an extraordinary investment. The turnaround program took a number of years and was extremely successful. We rebuilt both the property and the hotel's reputation in the community. Once remodeled and repositioned, the hotel reached both high occupancy and high rates. Eventually, we added a 43-unit, all-suite addition on the site.

About four years after acquiring the hotel, a huge oil boom began in North Dakota in the Bakken oil fields. The hotel became even more successful than we ever expected.

Benefit to Land Owner:

The Land Owner received a substantial amount of cash plus the commercial land in North Carolina.

The Land Owner no longer had to worry about the long-term success or failure of the hotel.

Benefit to Hotel Operator:

The Hotel Operator salvaged their investment in the hotel by receiving the adjacent land.

The Hotel Operator also received sufficient cash to pay off the accumulated debts of the hotel operation.

Key Points

Using the land as a down payment strategy allows a buyer to acquire property and reduce the amount of cash required in the purchase. Without the land, in many cases the buyer simply would not be able to make a purchase work at all. The land allows a buyer to stretch capital.

The land can be anywhere: next-door or halfway around the world. As with any property, full disclosure and due diligence are required.

What happens if you make an offer using land as a down payment and the seller rejects your offer? You could ask the seller to accept the contract contingent upon a sale of the land for cash and seller financing, or you could ask the seller to accept a note secured by the land as part of the down payment.

As you can see, the successful use of one creative financing approach can then open the door for the use of one or more additional strategies in the same transaction. The creative financing strategies can be used together to create the necessary level of benefits for all of the parties involved.

PROFESSIONAL SERVICES AS A DOWN PAYMENT

STRATEGY

A potential buyer who cannot come up with a sufficient down payment to purchase property can also offer professional services as a down payment.

This strategy has hundreds of possible variations. Examples of professional services could include legal fees, accounting, architectural services, construction, electrician services, painting, and interior design. Frankly, the possibilities are endless.

Furthermore, this approach can be used even when the buyer or buyers have only handyman skills. In most cases, they do not have to be licensed to perform general maintenance services, particularly if the work they are doing is on the house they are acquiring.

The approach typically (but not always) requires that the seller be able to use the professional services in their business or personal life.

RESIDENTIAL EXAMPLE

An acquaintance from a local real estate investment club was offering a house for sale at $109,000. Comparable reflected that the price was reasonable for the neighborhood, but the interior condition was only average. Other houses in the neighborhood were selling, but they were in pristine condition. The market for houses requiring substantial upgrades was very slow, as Buyers were looking for homes that were move-in ready.

The acquaintance (now Seller) located a potential Buyer who liked the house. However, the potential Buyer did not have anything for a down payment. The potential Buyer had rented an older home for several years.

He had a good job as a plumber. With a large family, he had been unable to accumulate sufficient savings to buy his own house.

The Seller continued to try to sell the house on the general market. When he was telling me about the trouble of finding a buyer for the house, my friend told me about the plumber but lamented that, unfortunately, the plumber had no money for a down payment. It was then I suggested he take plumbing services in lieu of cash.

SOLUTION

My friend decided to propose that the plumber give him $15,000 worth of future plumbing services as a down payment on the house. My friend (Seller) had a number of rental houses that he had been acquiring to fix up and resell. He could easily use a plumber's services on those properties. He would only have to accommodate the plumber's schedule of working outside the normal business hours of his regular job.

The Seller made the offer to sell the house to the Buyer subject to the Buyer making a down payment of $15,000 cash.

He also wrote a contract for services to hire the Buyer (Plumber) to do work and paid him $15,000 in cash in advance on his services and included a minimum number of hours per week under the contract. The down payment on the house and the payment in advance for the services contract then would close on the same day (simultaneously).

With the down payment and his steady job, the plumber easily qualified for a $97,000 loan to purchase the house. When he closed the purchase of the house, he also had saved enough cash for the closing costs of approximately $3,000.

PROFESSIONAL SERVICES AS A DOWN PAYMENT

SUMMARY OF TRANSACTION

Step 1: Purchase of plumbing services in advance

Seller → Pays $15,000 for plumbing services to the Buyer (Plumber)

Buyer (Plumber) → Receives prepaid services contract from the Seller

Step 2: Close on the sale of the house

Buyer (Plumber) → Pays $12,000 down payment for the house

Buyer (Plumber) → Pays $3,000 in closing costs

Buyer (Plumber) → Receives $97,000 loan secured by the house being purchased

Buyer (Plumber) → Pays $97,000 balance to the Seller

Seller → Deeds house to the Buyer (Plumber)

BENEFITS

Benefit to Buyer (Plumber):

The Buyer (Plumber) was able to buy a great house to accommodate his large family.

The Buyer (Plumber) had a structured a way of earning the down payment on the house.

Benefit to Seller (my friend):

The Seller (my friend) sold a property for full price in a slow market. In fact, if he had priced the house to sell quickly, he would have taken a substantial discount to get the house sold. By using professional services as a down payment, it could be said that the plumbing credits were a bonus to the Seller.

The Seller (my friend) also had a plumber on call to service his rental and for sale properties.

Commercial or Investment Example

A group of investors owned a parcel of undeveloped land in Arkansas. The land was located on the outskirts of a medium-sized town along the only major highway. The group of investors as owners planned to develop the land themselves and sell individual sites for a substantial profit. They had planned the sites for six commercial lots, all with highway access.

There was only one problem. The land required substantial grading in order to be made ready for sale. Since the cost of the utilities required would take all of the budgeted money the investors were able to invest in the project, they were short of the money for grading.

Solution

One member of the investor group approached a large, local grading company that owned a substantial amount of grading equipment and employed a large number of people.

The owners offered a simple proposal. The owners would deed one of the parcels of land free and clear to the grading company in return for the grading of the entire site. Although the value of the individual site once graded and improved was higher than the expected cost of the grading, it would allow the owners to avoid having to borrow money for the work.

The grading company determined that they could do the work with their existing crew and equipment between the other planned jobs they had scheduled. They would also still be able to meet the timetable of the owners.

The two parties negotiated an agreement and placed the deed to one of the six lots in escrow until the grading work was complete. In this way, both the Seller and the Buyer were protected in the event of any disagreements between the parties.

Summary of Transaction

Step 1: Transfer of lots to Grading Company

Owners → Place deed to one lot in escrow for grading

Step 2: Grading Company performs grading work

Grading Company → Performs the grading work on the entire site

Escrow Company → Releases the deed to the Grading Company

Owners → Sell the remainder of the lots to be developed

Owners → Make a profit on the sale of the remaining lots

Grading Company → Makes a profit by obtaining a lot worth more than the cost of the grading

Benefits

Benefits to Owners:

Owners receive grading work on the entire property without a cash outlay

Owners make a profit on the sales of the remaining commercial lots

Owners complete the job without taking out a loan

Benefits to Grading Company:

Grading Company buys commercial land at a substantial discount

Grading Company uses their existing overhead costs for purchase

Grading Company puts crews to work in slow times

KEY POINTS

Using professional services as a down payment, any buyer with valuable skills can parlay them into a down payment on real estate. This can be especially useful in times where there is some excess capacity of skills and products. Imagine what could be used as a down payment: legal services, manufacturing capacity, excess inventory, recreational vehicles, or even gift certificates. There are an endless number of possibilities.

The decision to accept the professional service credit as a down payment requires an analysis of the risk versus the reward of the transaction. In this analysis, you would look at the possible risks of the transaction. For example, a buyer could simply walk away from the obligation to provide the professional services, or the buyer may be unavailable when the seller of the property needs those services the most, or the two might have a disagreement concerning the quality of the services being delivered.

A potential seller would compare those risk factors to the projected rewards. For example, a quick sale may be more important than the total price or, the expected price discount required to sell the property conventionally may be too high, or the cash needed by the seller in the transaction may be necessary for an immediate financial requirement.

Once the seller evaluates the risks and the rewards, the seller will be required to make a decision to do the transaction in that form or not. That judgment call by the seller depends on many factors, including the reputation of the individual providing the professional services, how the parties know each other in the first place, and even the nature of the local market.

There are many ways to reduce the risk in the transaction. The buyer providing the professional services might provide additional collateral that would guarantee the performance of the services. A third party could guarantee the performance. Depending on the circumstances, the seller might place the deed to the property bring transferred into escrow until the professional services are provided.

The transfer or the receipt of the service credits may also be taxable at closing. Check with your CPA concerning your particular treatment.

DOWN PAYMENT EQUALS FREE AND CLEAR PROPERTY

STRATEGY

When buying a property with cash down and seller financing, you could
ask for a portion of the property being purchased to be delivered free and
clear of loans in return for the down payment.

When a buyer purchases a property that is divisible, he or she can offer a
cash down payment and then request carry-back financing, with a twist.
The twist is for the buyer to ask for a portion of the property to be delivered free and clear of the carry-back financing as consideration for the
down payment.

RESIDENTIAL EXAMPLE

An older couple had a house "for sale by owner" in a relatively mature
subdivision. The house was larger than other homes in the neighborhood,
with four bedrooms and three full baths. The house was also in excellent
condition.

The property consisted of two legally platted lots. The house was built on
only one of those two lots, with the other lot vacant with its own address
and opening for a future driveway.

The total asking price was $160,000. An average house in the neighbor-
hood with three bedrooms would normally appraise for the $160,000
asking price, but the market for that type of property was spotty, with
infrequent sales. Many homebuyers were seeking out newer homes in
new subdivisions on the outskirts of town.

While the Sellers were highly motivated to sell due to an illness in the family, they were not completely desperate. On the other hand, they had offered the property for a long time with no written contracts; they were anxious to get it over with and sell the property.

The Buyer was an opportunity-driven investor looking to make a profit though buying and selling. While this was not a deeply discounted property, the Buyer sensed an opportunity. The question was how to buy the house and make it worthwhile.

SOLUTION

The Buyer knew that the lots in the neighborhood were worth $25,000 each and that the house would appraise and eventually sell for somewhere near $170,000.

The Buyer and Seller signed two purchase contracts. One contract was for the house itself at $140,000 cash with a sixty-day closing. The Buyer also got the right to extend the closing for an additional thirty days for $5,000 additional earnest money. This would give the Buyer plenty of time to find another Buyer for the house at a price of $170,000. The second contract was for the sale of the vacant lot for $5,000 cash. Each contract was contingent on the simultaneous closing of the other contract.

A backup plan the Buyer immediately implemented was to apply to a local bank for a loan in the event that a resale could not be closed within the sixty-day or ninety-day period. Based upon the bank's appraisal and the strong financial statement of the Buyer, the Buyer was approved for a $120,000 one-year loan secured by the house. This backup loan gave the Buyer added confidence that a profitable transaction could be realized.

Simultaneously, the Buyer began an aggressive marketing program, including advertising the property online and through the network of local businesses with employees who might want to move into the neighbor-hood. The existing Sellers had not undertaken these actions.

As a result of the Buyer's creative marketing, he was able to find a new Buyer for the house at a purchase price of $165,000. The Buyer also sold the adjacent lot to a local builder at a discount cash price of $18,000. In total, the Buyer's gross resale price was $183,000 (the $165,000 sale of the house, plus the $18,000 sale of the adjacent lot). After accounting for the total purchase price of $145,000 ($140,000 for the house and $5,000 for the lot), the gross profit was $38,000, a very handsome profit.

The Sellers got an all-cash sale and relief from their money worries about the house.

SUMMARY OF TRANSACTION

Step 1: Buyer closes on the purchase of the house

Buyer → Pays $140,000 cash for house

Buyer → Pays $5,000 cash for lot

Seller → Gives deed to Buyer for house

Step 2: Buyer simultaneously closes on sale of house and sale of lot

Buyer → Sells house for $165,000 cash

Buyer → Sells adjacent lot for $18,000 cash

Buyer → Nets $38,000 profit

BENEFITS

Benefits to Buyer:

The Buyer negotiated a good purchase price and made an excellent profit.

The Buyer was able to find a nearly full-price Buyer because of the amount of time negotiated in the contracts.

The Buyer had the opportunity to execute a solid backup plan as well

Benefits to Sellers:

The Sellers received all cash to deal with the illness in the family.

The Sellers received peace of mind by resolving the sale of the house.

Commercial or Investment Example

In early January one year, a Colorado Hospital Group announced the merger of the operational departments of several hospitals in the greater Denver area. Because of the merger, the Hospital Group decided to close one smaller, older hospital in Denver. By closing that hospital, the Hospital Group planned to reallocate patient services to their remaining hospitals and save millions of dollars every year.

Furthermore, the Hospital Group would receive a large closure payment from the federal government if they sold the facility before the end of the calendar year. The closure payments were the federal government's incentive to consolidate hospitals and increase efficiency, thereby reducing costs.

Also included in the sale was a small, adjacent, medical office building that had many medical offices leased to doctors and other medical business uses. Most of the tenants of the medical office building were not planning to relocate. The building itself was older, but it had been well maintained and was in excellent condition. Accordingly, the building produced a very nice cash flow after paying all operating expenses.

The Hospital Group decided to offer the older hospital building and the office building for sale at a price of $4,000,000. The discount price was motivated by the desire to close a sale by the end of the year and qualify for the substantial federal closure payment. In February, the hospital group listed the property by employing a large national real estate brokerage company.

The property remained on the market for a number of months with no offers. The local competing hospitals were all in a strategy of consolida-

CREATIVE DOWN PAYMENTS

tion, not acquisition. Expansion plans for those other hospitals were all confined to new construction adjacent to existing facilities. By October, the Seller was highly motivated to close a sale.

SOLUTION

A real estate friend of mine named Ted was highly interested in the property. He planned to create a medical complex from the property and rent out space to doctors and clinics.

The price was great—$4,000,000 for a large building with significant medical improvements plus the medical office building. He had also determined that the medical office building could be easily subdivided from the overall property and financed separately. It could also be deeded separately in a sale.

While there was a substantial profit potential, the purchase price was way beyond my friend's ready cash.

To acquire the property, the Buyer (Ted):

1. Offered the Seller a $500,000 cash down payment;

2. Requested that the Seller deliver title to the medical office building (worth approximately $500,000) free and clear of all encumbrances;

3. Requested that the Seller provide seller financing by accepting a $1,500,000 carry-back note secured by the remainder of the hospital property alone.

The Buyer (Ted) arranged financing for the medical office building at a local bank for $350,000. That meant that Ted then only needed $150,000 to acquire the entire property. My friend raised the funds for the down payment from a few investors and completed the purchase once the hospital's attorneys had approved all of the required paperwork.

Once acquired, the Buyer rented the hospital facilities floor by floor to a number of tenants. In fact, the hospital group leased back several floors temporally for a specialty facility. In the process, Ted created significant cash flow for himself and for his investors. Ted turned the $150,000 down payment into a substantial profit when he sold the converted hospital and the medical office building a few years later.

SUMMARY OF TRANSACTION

Step 1: Buyer (Ted) closes on the purchase of the hospital and the medical office building

Buyer (Ted) → Buys the hospital and the medical office building for $4,000,000

Buyer (Ted)→ Gives a $500,000 cash down payment

Buyer (Ted) → Gives a deed to the Buyer (Ted) for the medical office building

Buyer (Ted) → Borrows $350,000 from the bank, secured by the medical office building

Buyer (Ted)→ Gives a $3,500,000 first mortgage secured only by the hospital building

Seller → Gives a deed to the Buyer (Ted) for the hospital

Buyer (Ted)→ Pays $350,000 cash from the bank loan or the closing (as shown in step 1 above)

Step 2: Ownership/sale phase

Buyer (Ted) → Rents hospital building and office building, creating cash flow

Buyer (Ted) → Sells hospital building and office building for substantial profit

BENEFITS

Benefits to Buyer (Ted):

The Buyer acquired a large property with a small down payment.

The Buyer also turned a low down payment into a substantial profit.

Benefits to Seller (Hospital Group):

The Seller (Hospital Group) sold the hospital, which was an asset they could no longer use.

The Seller (Hospital Group) also received a substantial closure payment that was even more significant than the sales price or terms.

ANOTHER COMMERCIAL / INVESTMENT EXAMPLE

Dan Murphy of Chicago, Illinois, shares the following example that is an extension of down payment equals free and clear property.

He calls the formula "Divide and Conquer." Often when his group buys a piece of investment property, some additional unpaved land goes with the property. In six separate occasions over the years, the group has subdivided such a property into two pieces prior to going out for financing. When lenders look at investment properties, they are looking at the income stream to determine value. Even if the land were included in the appraisal, the appraiser would attribute no significant additional value to the property unless it was a separate parcel. Once the parcel with the building is subdivided from the vacant land parcel, we take the parcel with the building out for financing. The lender secures his loan on the parcel with the building and the income stream and you are left with a vacant parcel free and clear of any liens. In the past the group has then sold the newly created vacant parcel or put a first mortgage against the parcel and used those funds as the down payment on the parcel with the building on it, ending up with a property that is 100 percent financed.

One example is a shopping center on twelve acres that was under contract for $3,200,000.

During the due diligence, Murphy's group created a ten-acre survey for the building and parking, and a two-acre survey for extra land. Based on the income, the center on ten acres appraised for $3,200,000. The two-acre vacant parcel was then sold for $800,000, which was the required 25 percent down payment on the shopping center on ten acres. Thus, Murphy and his associates achieved 100 percent financing.

While it does not work on every transaction with extra land, it is a great way to build equity and net worth. In the scenario above, if Murphy's group had financed the shopping center in a traditional manner, they would have put 25 percent down and had a 75 percent loan to value. The two-acre parcel would have fallen out of the transaction unencumbered and added $800,000 in net worth or value to the shopping center.

Dan Murphy's example would be equally relevant to many other types of properties, for example, a house located on two platted lots, a shopping center with potential outparcels, or an apartment building with extra land for future buildings.

Every transaction is situational—that is, based upon the circumstances of the potential site, the owners, the lenders, and the municipality. Just keep in mind to look for opportunities to split off land not directly germane to the original purchase. If you wait until after the transaction is closed, lenders may be extremely unlikely to release an excess parcel of land from the financing. It is best to negotiate this at the time of the original purchase.

KEY POINTS

In the "Down Payment Equals Free and Clear" strategy, the Buyer ends up with (or creates as Dan Murphy demonstrated) a free and clear asset that can either be financed or sold. This both reduces the net cash down payment required for the purchase and increases the percentage yield on investment.

A buyer using this strategy would want to negotiate receiving a free and clear asset that is desirable from a potential lender's or a buyer's point of view. It does no good to receive an asset free and clear that lacks any real marketability. Therefore the configuration of the building or land parcel, the physical road access to the site, or the utility connection are examples of items to be carefully considered in the equation to split off the excess property using this strategy.

APPLY THE DOWN PAYMENT TO THE MONTHLY DEBT SERVICE

STRATEGY

Beginning with the idea that everything is negotiable, even the use of the down payment can be considered negotiable. One way to apply that principal is to negotiate having part of the down payment be applied to future monthly note payments.

That down payment could be applied to reduce both principal payments or interest payments or both. In one transaction where I was the Seller, I gave the Buyer twelve payment vouchers for the first year's monthly payments. We were using an escrow account with a title company, so it made it easy for the title company to track the payments. In this case, I wanted to have regular monthly payments coming from some source to make the seller-financed note more saleable in the open market.

In practical terms, the Buyer could hold those vouchers until a month when they did not have the money to make a payment, or the Buyer could give those payment vouchers all at once at the beginning so there was no question as to the payment being made on time.

 Another way to manage this could be to simply state in the promissory note that certain payments were to come out of the down payment delivered to Seller.

Whichever way it is handled, it is a way to deal with the gap between the Seller wanting payments and the Buyer not wanting to make payments. Again, there are times when the form of the transaction is sometimes more important than the substance of the transaction. Changing the form can be used to satisfy the goals of all parties to the transaction.

Both the Buyer and the Seller in such a transaction would want the application of the vouchers to be clearly set forth in the closing documents.

RESIDENTIAL EXAMPLE

A remodeling contractor was considering buying a vacant house in Dallas to remodel and resell. The property required substantial remodeling and several months to do the work and resell the house. The Seller was a relocation company that wanted a quick sale. Someone in the company had made a big mistake in accepting an appraisal that showed a market value much higher than it should have been.

The relocation company had already paid off the original owner. The delay in sorting out their mistake cost them both a substantial amount of money and the wasted time when the property was listed at a much higher price.

Fortunately, the relocation company quickly became realistic about the condition of the property and what would be required for a resale. The original owner was a corporate client that was a big customer, so they were prepared to absorb their mistake. They also had become realistic about the real market value of the house. They were prepared to discount substantially to get the house sold quickly. Said another way, the relocation company was highly flexible and wanted this property off their inventory.

The purchase price was $115,000. The property had no existing loan. The relocation company wanted all cash.

SOLUTION

The contractor offered to buy the house at the full asking price of

$115,000 and give a $15,000 cash down payment. He asked that the relocation company provide $100,000 in seller financing for six months at no interest so that he had time to remodel the property. The contractor also offered to close the purchase of the house from the relocation company in ten days. In that way, the contractor would have little additional out of pocket carrying costs.

Furthermore, the contractor offered to pay $1,000 per month additional during the six month seller financing period, but the contractor also required that 100 percent of the payments be applied to the principal balance of the carry-back financing.

Although the relocation company did not like the idea of giving any carry-back financing, especially at no interest, they were motivated to sell quickly. The contractor was firm in the terms of his offer. The relocation company accepted the offer and closed the transaction.

Four months later, the contract had remodeled the property at an out-of-pocket cost of approximately $20,000. In this case, the contractor personally performed a great deal of the physical work of remodeling the property himself. Before the expiration of the six-month term of the seller financing, the contractor resold the house for $185,000. The contractor paid off the seller financed note of $100,000 to the relocation company and made a $50,000 gross profit.

Summary of Transaction

Step 1: Close on Purchase of House

Buyer (Contractor) → Buys the house for $115,000

Buyer (Contractor) → Gives the Seller $100,000 note and mortgage for 6 months

Buyer (Contractor) → Gives the Seller $15,000 down payment

Buyer (Contractor) → Pays $1,000 per month toward the principal balance of the seller financing (no interest)

Seller → Gives the Buyer (Contractor) a deed to the house

Step 2: Remodeling and resale

Buyer (Contractor) → Remodels the house for $20,000

Buyer (Contractor) → Sells the house for $185,000

Buyer (Contractor) → Recoups the $15,000 down payment

Buyer (Contractor) → Recoups $20,000 remodeling costs

Buyer (Contractor) → Pays off note to relocation company (no net interest)

Buyer (Contractor) → Makes a $50,000 gross profit (before cost of selling the house to a new owner)

BENEFITS

Benefits to Buyer (Contractor):

The Buyer (Contractor) made a $50,000 profit.

The Buyer (Contractor) avoided any "out-of-pocket" payments for six months.

Benefits to Seller:

The Relocation Company quickly minimized their loss through the quick sale (even though they did not receive full payment for six months).

Commercial or Investment Example

A friend of mine was buying land for future development on the outskirts of Wichita, Kansas. In this case, my friend had raised funds for the down payment from a joint venture with two of his partners from previous projects. The plan was to hold the land as a long-term investment and develop or sell it when the market was right.

My friend and the investors, however, did not want to have ongoing monthly carrying costs to hold the land (interest, taxes, maintenance, etc.).

Solution

My friend offered a large down payment to the Seller. However, he required that a portion of the down payment apply in advance to the first thirty-six of the monthly note payments. In this way, my friend would have no payments on the note for the first three years.

Summary of Transaction

Step 1: Close on the purchase of the land

Buyer → Gives Seller a large down payment

Buyer → Receives seller financing for the balance

Buyer → Has no payments for three years

Buyer → Has time without pressure to subdivide and sell individual parcels of the land

Benefits

Benefit to Buyer:

The Buyer reduced the risk of losing the property due to some unforeseen circumstance arising with her or the investors.

The Buyer did not have to continually raise the carrying costs from the investors or from discounted sales of the individual parcels.

Benefit to Investors:

Investors had upfront clarity about what their real financial commitment would be for the first three years.

The Investors had a solid investment not subject to day-to-day financial pressures.

Benefit to Seller:

Seller received greater security from the larger down payment.

The Buyer's approach to reducing risk also protected the Seller providing the Seller financing.

KEY POINTS

There are many ways to apply all or part of the down payments to reduce or eliminate certain future payments.

Changing the form of a transaction by apply the down payment in a creative way can benefit all parties to the transaction.

ADDITIONAL COLLATERAL FOR DOWN PAYMENT

STRATEGY

When the Buyer cannot raise the normal down payment to purchase a property, the Buyer can use additional collateral to provide increased security to a lender. This is also known as cross-collateralization.

Whether the lender is an individual or a financial institution, this approach can be effective to satisfy the lender's security concerns.

Additional collateral or cross collateralization refers to the assigning of additional assets to secure a loan. This assignment of additional assets to increase the loan security might be done not only to provide additional security in the event of a default, but also to meet certain regulatory requirements of the lending institution. The additional collateral can be documented in one of two ways: first, by means of a separate security agreement for each piece of collateral or second, by including the additional collateral in the primary security agreement.

Regardless, the borrower should always negotiate a predetermined method of obtaining a release of the additional collateral. This could be a certain loan-to-value ratio of the primary collateral based upon an appraisal, or a sum certain principal reduction of the original loan, or even a certain percentage of sale proceeds of the additional collateral. Each of these is defined in the glossary at the end of this book.

Whatever method is used to calculate the release of the additional collateral as security, again, it is a good principle to always negotiate some predetermined way to obtain a release of the recorded mortgage on the property held as additional collateral.

RESIDENTIAL EXAMPLE

Assume you are buying a rental house from an investor. The house is $80,000 and you have offered $8,000 as a cash down payment and asked the owners to finance the balance of $72,000. With a minimal down payment, you may find the Sellers will be worried about your ability to repay the amount of any seller financing. They might say, "That's not a big enough down payment," or "What if you default?" It is usually is not a matter of the money itself, but rather the risk to themselves that they perceive because of a small down payment.

SOLUTION

In that event, you could ask them if they will accept something else as additional collateral for the seller financing. That could be anything, such as the equity in another house, or a piece of land that you may own. In the case of default, they still would have the security of two properties instead of just one. When you own any kind of property and do not think it has much value, do not dismiss it as an option for additional collateral. As I noted in an earlier example, it is not about the money; it is about the perception of risk.

Anything can be used as substitute collateral in this approach. Items could include houses, land, commercial property, automobiles, jewelry, stocks, bonds, artwork, and certificates of deposit—literally anything!

If you are the one providing the additional collateral, just remember to have the loan documents drafted to include the right to get a release of the property used as additional collateral once you pay down the loan sufficiently. The criteria for the release of the additional collateral do not have to be a 100 percent payoff of the loan. It is all a matter of negotiation.

For example, you could negotiate for a release of the additional collateral when there is a reduction of 50 percent of the loan principal, or with payment of a specific amount of money, or when the property used as the primary collateral for the loan is appraised at a certain market value. Again, the method of calculating the release requirement is all a matter of negotiation.

SUMMARY OF TRANSACTION

Step 1: Close on the purchase of the house

Buyer → Gives the Seller an $8,000 down payment

Buyer → Gives the Seller a note for $72,000

Seller → Gives the Buyer a deed to the rental house

Buyer → Gives the Seller a first mortgage on the rental house

Buyer → Gives the Seller additional collateral on other land

BENEFITS

Benefits to Buyer:

Buyer acquires the new rental property with desired cash down payment.

The Buyer leverages existing assets to keep cash down payment low.

Benefits to Seller:

The Seller gets additional security for the purchase from the seller financing provided.

The Seller gets the property SOLD!

COMMERCIAL OR INVESTMENT EXAMPLE

Jessica Richer, a commercial real estate broker in upstate New York, had a listing on a vacant restaurant that a local bank had taken back in foreclosure. While the property was in a location slightly off the main commercial street where other restaurants were located, the kitchen equipment and furniture were in good condition and highly usable.

The real estate brokers representing the bank had offered the vacant restaurant for sale for a long time with no activity. National chains typically find it difficult and costly to convert a restaurant to their design standards, even if the restaurant happens to meet their location standards. Therefore, few national restaurants were interested in the property.

Jessica had located a successful local, family-owned restaurant operator that wanted to acquire the vacant restaurant in order to open a second unit. The family had operated a popular local ethnic restaurant for many years and had a solid reputation in the community. The existing restaurant produced good cash flow and a solid basis for expanding the family business. A new generation of family members was coming of age and the family wanted to make a place for them, hence, the interest in a second location.

Although the bank was asking $800,000 for the restaurant, the family calculated that they could only afford $600,000 based on the location. The secondary location would require more promotion and advertising to establish the business. As a result of their analysis, the family offered $600,000. The bank reluctantly agreed to that price.

Once a price was verbally agreed upon, Jessica turned her attention to financing. Independent restaurants are among the most difficult types of property to finance. The failure rate is high and the borrowers are frequently financially marginal. In addition, a restaurant that twice turns dark or vacant is doubly hard to resell. The most likely source of financing was the bank as the Seller, but the loan still needed to meet normal lending requirements and regulatory oversight.

The bank was willing to provide financing based upon 70 percent of the purchase price, or $420,000 based upon a $600,000 purchase price. That would have required a down payment of $180,000, plus money for remodeling and operating capital.

After calculating the funds needed for that remodeling and operating capital, the Buyer could only come up with about $75,000 for the down payment. That would require a loan of $525,000, or 87.5 percent of the cost. The bank's credit committee and federal regulators would not approve that loan and the reduced down payment. Furthermore, the bank felt they could not reduce the price any further. The bank and the family seemed to be at an impasse.

SOLUTION

Jessica had participated in one of my training classes and knew Creative Real Estate Principle #5: "It's About the People, Not Just the Property." That requires an understanding of all of the people involved in a transaction, which includes both the buyer and the seller. Creative real estate solutions require that you understand the motivation and options people have in order to create and implement effective solutions.

Through in-depth questioning, Jessica determined that the family-owned restaurant operator owned a piece of land on the other side of town that they had purchased years earlier for a future restaurant location. The land was worth about $300,000 and was free and clear of any loans. However, the lending environment for a new restaurant loan was not supportive of developing it at that time. Federally regulated banks were under extreme pressure to substantially reduce the number of commercial loans issued, and local banks were extremely selective as to where they would risk their funds. Developing the site for a new restaurant was just not a viable option at that time. However, Jessica saw that the land could help the family purchase of the vacant restaurant now.

With Jessica's help, the family's attorney drafted a real estate contract that provided for a down payment of $75,000 with a $525,000 loan for the site owned by the bank. The family offered to provide the parcel of land they already owned as additional collateral for the loan.

The resulting loan of $525,000 secured by the $900,000 in property (the $600,000 restaurant and $300,000 in land) represented a loan to value ratio of about 58 percent ($525,000 divided by $900,000).

This more than satisfied the bank's underwriting requirements.

The Seller (Bank) agreed to the purchase price and loan terms subject to an appraisal of both properties and contingent upon the Buyer moving all of their existing operating and savings accounts to the bank providing the financing.

In addition to the promissory note for $525,000, the bank elected to have a single document recording the security provided by the Buyer (called a security instrument) for both parcels. The Buyer, with Jessica's counseling, negotiated a release provision with the bank for the mortgage on the vacant land once the principal balance on the entire loan was reduced to $420,000. That represented a 70 percent loan-to-cost ratio against the $600,000 purchase price, which met the underwriting requirements of the bank.

With those provisions in place, they closed the transaction and financing for the sale of the restaurant property.

SUMMARY OF TRANSACTION

Step 1: Close on the purchase of the vacant restaurant

Buyer (Restaurant Operator Family) → Agrees to buy the vacant restaurant for $600,000

Buyer (Restaurant Operator Family) → Gives Seller (Bank) cash down payment of $75,000

Buyer (Restaurant Operator Family): → Gives Seller (Bank) note for $525,000

Seller (Bank) → Gives Buyer (Restaurant Operator Family) the deed to the vacant restaurant

Buyer (Restaurant Operator Family) → Gives the Bank a $525,000 promissory note and first mortgage, secured by both the vacant restaurant and the free and clear land parcel

BENEFITS

Benefit to Buyer (Restaurant Operator Family):

The Buyer obtained a second location to expand their restaurant operations.

The Buyer was able to use their reputation in the community to expand both their operations and their cash flow.

The Buyer could use excess cash flow from restaurant operations in the years ahead to pay down the loan further and eventually build their third restaurant on the vacant land they already owned.

Benefit to Seller (Bank):

The Seller disposed of a foreclosed asset that was difficult to sell (vacant restaurant).

The Seller satisfied the underwriting requirements concerning minimum loan to value requirements.

The Seller received monthly interest on a well-secured loan.

The Seller obtained a new customer's business checking and savings accounts.

Benefits to Broker (Jessica):

The Broker earned a substantial real estate fee.

The Broker impressed the bank and the client with her creativity.

The Broker secured a long-term client who was grateful for her assistance in obtaining the restaurant on favorable terms.

KEY POINTS

Providing additional collateral on a loan provides increased security to a lender.

This assignment of additional assets to increase the loan security might be done not only to provide additional security in the event of a default, but also to meet certain regulatory requirements of the lending institution.

Whenever one adds additional collateral to secure a loan, always negotiate some predetermined way to obtain a release of the recorded mortgage on the property held as additional collateral.

BORROW A PROPERTY AS COLLATERAL FOR A LOAN

One method of making yourself or someone else more credit-worthy for a loan is to borrow a property for collateral. This could be for additional collateral or as the sole collateral.

Today, more than ever, banks require collateral. No longer is a personal signature without collateral sufficient to meet either a lender's or a federal agency's underwriting requirements. Quality collateral is vital.

Even hard money lenders today work primarily from the quality of the collateral, not the personal guarantees of the borrower.

Stocks, bonds, mortgages, and certificates of deposit all have a high collateral priority. If those are available as collateral for a loan, a loan is much easier to negotiate.

Yet, one thing that is in plentiful supply is real estate. As a hard asset, real estate makes an excellent vehicle for providing collateral for a loan.

Because of regulatory issues and comfort issues, lenders work best with collateral that is within close proximity to the lender themselves. While real estate is plentiful throughout the world, the real estate that you use as collateral for a loan is best if lenders can easily inspect it for themselves.

RESIDENTIAL EXAMPLE

Imagine that you are building your expertise and your portfolio of rentals. You locate three houses for a total price of $300,000 that are available at a good price from some out-of-state owners. You are convinced you can re-model and make a large profit on the purchase and remodel of the houses.

While the out-of-state owners are knowledgeable real estate Investors, they have been unable to effectively manage their properties long dis-tance. Two of the three houses are vacant and all three have some de-ferred maintenance. The owners want to focus on their other investments in their home state.

The owners want to sell, but also want a good price. They are realistic enough to know that they may have to provide seller financing in order to get their price, but they want 15 percent in down payment.

The only problem is you do not have the 15 percent down payment, which totals $45,000.

SOLUTION

You could find an investor who has assets that could be used as additional collateral. Offer the investor a partnership interest in the houses if they will put up some of their assets as additional collateral for the seller financing.

For instance, you could offer the investor a percentage of the net profits after the payoff of all loans and costs, and after the release of his addi-tional collateral.

You should also ask for individual notes and mortgages on each of the three houses. In that way, when you eventually sell an individual house, you are not required to pay off the entire loan to sell one property. If the Seller insisted on a single note and mortgage encompassing all three houses, you should insist on a way to release any one house with a payoff of a certain defined or definable amount of the loan. This is really also in the best interest of the Sellers eventually receiving the timely return of their seller-financed note.

Summary of Transaction

Step 1: Close on purchase of houses

Buyer → Agrees to buy the three houses for $300,000 from the Seller

Buyer → Give Seller three separate notes of $100,000 ($300,000 total)

Buyer → Gives Seller individual first mortgages on each of the houses as security for the loan

Buyer → Gives Seller additional collateral on investor's property

Seller → Gives Buyer deed to houses

Step: 2 Ownership of the houses

Buyer → Takes possession of the three houses

Buyer → Cures the deferred maintained of each of the houses

Buyer → Finds tenants for each of the houses

Buyer → Owns and manages each of the three houses

Step 3: Sale of the individual houses

Buyer → Creates plan to sell one or more houses

Buyer → Makes the house(s) ready for sale

Buyer → Contracts to sell an individual house

Buyer → Closes the sale and pays the lender the required payment to release the house as collateral

BENEFITS

Benefits to the Buyer (You):

You get to acquire what could be a highly profitable investment with a minimal down payment.

You have structured the payoff criteria on the seller-financed in advance.

Benefits to the Sellers:

The Sellers receive an acceptable price by providing seller financing.

The Sellers receive sufficient collateral to ensure the full payment of amount of the seller financing.

Benefit to the Investor:

The Investor gets a percentage of a profitable investment with no money down by providing the additional collateral to make the seller financing acceptable to the out-of-state Sellers.

COMMERCIAL OR INVESTMENT EXAMPLE

In the 1980s, a small group of entrepreneurs that I was part of decided to open a chain of retail video stores in several states. The bank we wanted to work with was interested in the financing, as it also wanted to control the checking accounts from the business. However, the bank also wanted some hard assets as additional collateral. They had no interest in making loans to a group of entrepreneurs based solely on the members' credit or overall financial statements. Furthermore, the inventory for the business would not be readily saleable in an amount sufficient to repay any loan. The bank wanted hard assets.

The total cost of opening all of the stores was approximately $2,000,000. Between the members of our entrepreneurial group, we simply did not have the cash satisfy the bank equity requirements for a loan.

SOLUTION

A friend of one of our partners was an Investor who owned a parcel of land zoned for apartments. The land had an appraisal value of $1,200,000. However, the location was several miles beyond the prime development areas. New development was slowly proceeding in the direction of that site, but our friend's site would take several years to be ready for new apartments.

We offered the Investor an interest in the retail chain if he would pledge his land as additional collateral for our bank loan. We pointed out that he would be able to earn a monthly income from his share of the net cash flow (after debt payments) while he waited for the land to be ready for development. He agreed to the proposal. We had our attorneys draw up an agreement between the four principals of the video rental company and the owner of the land we were using as additional collateral.

The Bank made the loan of $2,000,000 for the construction, inventory, and operating capital for the new chain of retail stores, securing our loan by the leasehold improvements, the inventory, and the apartment land as additional collateral.

SUMMARY OF TRANSACTION

Step 1: Close on loan for development of stores

Buyers → Develop plan to development retail stores for $2,000,000

Investor → Puts up $1,200,000 land as additional collateral in exchange for an interest in the Limited Liability Corporation that we formed to own and operate the retail stores

Buyers → Give the Bank a security assignment of the stores, inventory, and operating capital as security for the loan

Bank → Makes loan of $2,000,000 for development costs

Step 2: The retail stores are developed and opened

The Limited Liability Corporation (that we formed) → Developed, opened, owned, and operated the retail stores

BENEFITS

Benefit to our Entrepreneurial Group:

We developed our retail stores using almost none of our own cash. The bank provided virtually all of the money.

Benefit to the Bank:

The Bank made a well-secured loan with the land provided by the Land

Owner as additional collateral.

The Bank also received the depository accounts from the business locations that we developed.

Benefit to the Land Owner:

The Land Owner received an annual cash return from the company cash flow for risking his land as the additional collateral. He received that annual cash flow until the release of the land as additional collateral.

The Land Owner also received a release of his land when we refinanced our loan a few years later.

KEY POINTS

One method of making yourself or someone else more credit-worthy for a loan is to borrow a property for collateral.

As a hard asset, real estate makes an excellent vehicle for providing collateral for a loan.

Because of regulatory issues and comfort issues, lenders work best with collateral that is within close proximity to the lender themselves.

DEPOSIT MONEY TO OBTAIN A LOAN

STRATEGY

Where financing is usually required and sometimes difficult to obtain, potential lenders will frequently make a loan if you deposit sufficient money into their bank. The bank uses both their general deposits and your deposits to make the loan.

General checking accounts gives banks fees from the checking accounts themselves, as well as providing money for the bank to use, usually costing them little or no interest. Certificates of Deposit give banks money for a predetermined period of time at very low interest costs. Both types of deposits provide the funds and reserves for making loans to other customers. The interest secured by real estate constitutes the bulk of earnings for many banks.

Sometimes the bank will require a pledge of the deposits in addition to the real estate. However, that is generally not the case. It depends upon all of the circumstances surrounding the property, the bank, and you.

RESIDENTIAL EXAMPLE

I had found a house to buy at a great price. The house was in terrible condition and needed a substantial amount of remodeling. I wanted to remodel the house myself and resell it.

After talking with the owner, I knew that the owners would accept $120,000 cash with a quick closing. I estimated the remodeling cost at $30,000 if I managed the remodeling myself. I estimated that I could resell the remodeled house for a gross price of $220,000.

To buy the house for all cash and to perform the remodeling, I needed financing. While I estimated that I could complete the remodeling in about sixty days, I wanted a cushion of time. I verbally asked my banker to make a six-month loan for 60 percent of the purchase price and I would put in the money for all of the remodeling.

My first thought was that this arrangement might be acceptable as the bank normally made loans on commercial properties at 70 percent of the total purchase price and remodeling costs. My banker told me that making the loan required a direct source of monthly interest payments from the property. While I protested that I could easily make those interest payments from my other income and that the remodeled house sale would be the ultimate source of repayment, my banker said that it would make no difference. He wanted to make the loan, but was subject to increasing underwriting requirements from his own bank and from federal regulators. I left our initial discussion with the clarity that I had to create an offer that proved this was a no-risk loan.

SOLUTION

I put myself in my banker's shoes. What was the real issue here?

I knew that banks were under increasing scrutiny from regulators to make safe loans and my banker did not want to make even a small loan that could be considered risky. Clearly, an alternate source of repayment was important to the Bank. How could I provide an alternate source of repayment if the house was not rented?

I proposed to the Bank *in writing* that they make a 70 percent loan (instead of a 60 percent loan I had verbally proposed). I then proposed that I create an escrow account and put the extra $12,000 (the difference between the two loan amounts) into that account. The Bank then could use the account to draw out the monthly interest payments in the event I did not pay them in a timely manner. They could also use the account to pay down the loan in the event I defaulted.

The banker readily agreed. The internal credit committee of the bank independently approved the loan as well.

It seems counter-intuitive that this would be a better solution for the Bank. After all, the escrow account would be created with their money. I was putting in no additional cash than I had proposed earlier. However, this was a case where the form of the transaction was important. The escrow account created that alternate source of repayment and satisfied the regulatory requirements and their own bank's credit standards.

At the closing, I received an $84,000 loan from the bank (70 percent of $120,000) and invested $36,000 for the balance of the purchase price. I paid a total of approximately $6,000 for closing costs on the purchase of the house.

Once I had closed the purchase of the house and received the loan from the bank, I remodeled the house and sold it as planned. The bank never had to access the escrow account. However, that escrow account served an important purpose in the loan transaction.

I ended up investing approximately $33,000 remodeling the house (not including my own sweat equity). I sold the house after four months for $214,000 with closing costs of approximately $10,000. This amount included a referral fee to a broker for sending a Buyer to me.

Ultimately, I made a gross profit of $40,500, as follows:

CALCULATION OF NET SALES PRICE

Sales Price	$214,000
Less: Closing Costs on Sale	-$10,000
Less: Remodeling Costs	-$33,000
Less: Carrying Costs	-$4,500
Net Sales Price	$166,500

CALCULATIONS OF NET PROFIT

Net Sales Price	$166,500
Less: Purchase Price	-$120,000
Less: Closing Costs of Purchase	-$6,000
Net Profit	$40,000

From the time I located the house until I closed the re-sale of the house was approximately six months. It took two months to close the purchase of the house and four months to remodel and sell it. Note that I was fortunate that I had negotiated a six-month loan term with the Bank.

I estimated that my *time* for locating, acquiring, financing, remodeling, and selling the house was worth about $15,000. After consideration of the valuation of my time and talent, I made a return on my *capital and the entrepreneurial risk* of $25,500 ($40,500 Net Profit less the $15,000 allocation for my time and talent).

This was, for me, a demonstration of a successful investment. I bought the house at the right price. I negotiated a good six-month loan with the bank. I reasonably estimated the remodeling costs. Finally, I sold the house for a profit yielding me both a return on my time and talent, as well as a return on my capital and the entrepreneurial risk.

SUMMARY OF TRANSACTION

Step 1: Close on purchase of the house

Buyer (me) → Invests $36,000 in the purchase of the house (30 percent of 120,000)

Buyer (me) → Borrows $84,000 from the Bank (70 percent of 120,000)

Buyer (me) → Creates and gives the Bank an assignment of a $12,000 escrow account

Buyer (me) → Pays the Seller $120,000 for the house

Buyer (me) → Pays the closing costs of approximately $6,000

Seller → Transfers the deed to the house to the Buyer

Step 2: Remodel and sale of the house

Buyer (me) → Invests $33,000 in the remodeling of the house

Buyer (me) → Sells the house for $214,000

Buyer (me) → Pays off the $84,000 loan

Buyer (me) → Pays closing costs of approximately $10,000

Buyer (me) → Receives the $12,000 held in the escrow account

Buyer (me) → Makes a net profit of $40,500

BENEFITS

Benefits to the Bank:

The Bank made a loan that satisfied their regulatory requirements and their own banks credit standards.

The Bank was able to make a loan to a good customer (me) and maintain our longstanding banking relationship.

The Bank received interest on the entire loan they made, but paid no interest on the escrow account. Therefore, they raised the real effective interest rate on the loan by receiving interest on the entire while paying no interest on the $12,000 portion of the loan that held in the escrow account

Benefit to Buyer (me):

The Buyer (me) received a loan that my banker could not otherwise have made.

The Buyer (me) cemented a valuable working relationship with my bank.

The Buyer (me) made a profit on buying, remodeling, and reselling the house.

COMMERCIAL OR INVESTMENT EXAMPLE

Larry Browning, a creative developer, investor, and broker from India-napolis, Indiana, was looking at acquiring a local shopping center where a major grocery store chain had just vacated the anchor space. The own-ers were out of Canada and had no ideas on how they would replace the grocery store chain as a tenant. However, Larry did not have a tenant or a loan to acquire and remodel the property.

SOLUTION

Larry was aware that a local hospital was looking for about 10,000 square feet of office space. He approached them about going into this center if he were able to acquire it. The discussions went further than that as he found out that they had some other needs for space.

He invited them to join his investment group to acquire the center and to enter into some long-term leases on spaces within the shopping center. In addition, the Hospital was a community leader and they were determined to bring a cinema operation to our local market.

Larry acquired the 70,000 square foot center for $2,300,000. He found out that the Hospital had many millions of dollars in local banks gaining short-term interest rates. He went to two local banks and asked them to make a $2,300,000 loan, promising that the Hospital would deposit $2,300,000 (compensating balance) in their Banks. They split the funds and the loans equally between the two Banks. The Banks were thrilled and indicated that they would pay the hospital whatever rate they wanted and then they would charge a spread on the loan at somewhere between a .5 percent and 1 percent. They agreed on a 3 percent interest rate on the loan and the hospital received 2.5 percent on their deposited funds. Essentially, the Banks made $11,500 net interest on money that the hospital deposited with them. The banks had no net cash invested in this loan.

The bottom line was that Larry's group had a shopping center free and clear of loans with an agreement with the Hospital that the Investment Group would pay the loan terms that were guaranteed by the deposited funds and it was at a below-market interest rate. In addition, the investment group entered into an agreement with a regional cinema operation to build out a ten-screen cinema in the former grocery store space. They entered into three leases with the hospital for a billing office, a sleep center, and a physical rehabilitation clinic.

After completion of the cinema build-out, the shopping center was full and flowing, providing about $250,000 in cash flow. This provided useful cash flow for Larry and his team. It also provided cash flow for the Hospital.

Later, the Hospital needed to release their deposited funds to build a cancer center, so Larry's group put a new first mortgage on the shopping center at a 2 percent interest rate.

The center has been a tremendous home run for all of the owners. It provided cash flow to the hospital without any risk of their money. Furthermore, it provided cash flow and eventual profit upon sale.

The loan was also a home run for the two Banks. They received net interest on money deposited by the Hospital.

Finally, the investment was a home run for Larry's investment group. They made a profit without investing any of their own capital. Furthermore, they strengthened their business relationship with the two Banks and the Hospital.

These net benefits to all the parties involved is what made the project come together in the first place and held the project together over its entire term.

Larry continues to look for new opportunities in which he can pledge compensating balances in order to make new acquisitions. This provides a means for parties who have large amounts of funds in banks or Certificates of Deposits to put those funds to work to either gain higher interest rates or make lots of money in new ventures like real estate.

SUMMARY OF TRANSACTION

Step 1: Close on purchase of the shopping center

Buyer (Investment Group) → Pays the Seller $2,300,000 for shopping center

Hospital → Deposits $2,300,000 into the Banks for 2.5 percent interest

Banks → Make a $2,300,000 loan to the Buyer for 3 percent interest

Buyer (Investment Group) → Invested $0 in the purchase of the shopping center

Step 2: Operation of the shopping center

Buyer (Investment Group) Leases space to a ten-screen cinema, a hospital billing office, a sleep center, and a physical rehabilitation clinic

Buyer (Investment Group) Remodels the shopping center for the new tenants

Buyer (Investment Group) Increases cash flow to $250,000 above the loan payment

Step 3: Refinancing of shopping center

Buyer (Investment Group) Refinances the shopping center with a new bank

Hospital → Withdraws the $2,300,000 in deposits from first two banks

BENEFITS

Benefit to the Hospital:

The Hospital used the power to move its money to become a part of the investment group.

The Hospital never risked any of its money in the process. The $2,300,000 in deposits was never pledged to the bank for the development loan.

The Hospital also contributed to the community by bringing into the neighborhood a much-desired cinema.

Benefit to the Developer (Larry Browning and Team):

The Developer received 100 percent financing for the project.

The Developer was able to use the tenancy of the Hospital as a cornerstone of the project's success.

The Developer made a very good cash flow and overall profit.

KEY POINTS

Where financing is usually required and sometimes difficult to obtain, potential lenders will frequently make a loan if you deposit sufficient money into their bank.

Sometimes the bank will require a pledge of the deposits in addition to the real estate. However, that is generally not the case. It all depends upon the circumstances surrounding the property, the bank, and you.

The use of compensating balances provides a means for parties who have large amounts of funds in banks or Certificates of Deposits to put those funds to work with low risk to either gain higher interest rate returns or make money in new ventures like real estate.

BORROW A CERTIFICATE OF DEPOSIT TO OBTAIN A LOAN

STRATEGY

In this section, we extend the "Compensating Balances" strategy from the prior section to include third-party sources of deposited funds. As an incentive for a financial institution to make a loan, you can entice a third party to place compensating balances into the bank. Those compensating balances might be in the form of checking accounts, savings accounts, or Certificates of Deposit.

RESIDENTIAL EXAMPLE

A builder who remodeled houses was considering buying a house from an older couple for $125,000 The Builder's plan was to remodel the house and then resell it. The older couple did not need a large house any longer as their children were all grown. The couple was also planning to retire soon and wanted to be out of the big house before they did that.

The house had been on the market for quite some time as the Sellers were intent on getting their price. However, these Sellers could afford to wait, as they were not under any pressure to sell quickly.

Although the house was located in a popular neighborhood, the house was dated and had not been remodeled in more than twenty years. Younger couples were moving into the area because of its image, but were only interested in move-in ready houses. The Buyer believed that the house would sell quickly with some upgrades, particularly to the bathrooms and kitchen. The builder estimated that those upgrade and remodeling costs would be approximately $30,000.

While the builder was clear he could make a strong profit on the house project, he did not have all of the money to both buy the house and complete the remodeling. The local bank was not enthusiastic about making him a loan to do so. His friends and recent investors were tapped out and had no money they wanted to invest.

SOLUTION

The Builder sat down with the Sellers of the house and made a simple proposal. He would buy the house for the full price of $125,000, but he wanted the Sellers to put $30,000 into a one-year Certificate of Deposit with a bank of the Builder's choosing. The Sellers were initially concerned about risking $30,000 of their money, but the Builder assured them the certificate of deposit would not be at risk in any way. All they had to do was promise that the certificate of deposit would not be cashed in for one year.

After a contract was drawn stating all of that in very clear terms and reviewed by the attorneys for the Buyer and the Seller, they all signed the contract.

The Builder took the contract and the cost estimates to their neighborhood bank. This was not simply a neighborhood branch of a big national bank. This was the main headquarters for a new, small bank that serviced this particular area. The Bank's loan officer was intrigued with the idea of both a neighborhood loan and a certificate of deposit with a resident of their target market.

The Builder asked for a $125,000 loan and agreed to put $30,000 additional into remodeling the house. After due consideration, requests for additional meetings, and submittal of additional documentation, the Bank agreed to make the loan.

If the first bank had not agreed to this arrangement, the Builder could have taken the contract o another bank. The Builder would then have to educate the Seller that an FDIC-insured Certificate of Deposit at one bank was equivalent to a Certificate of Deposit at another FDIC bank. In this example, that was not necessary, as the first bank liked the terms of the proposal.

Summary of Transaction

Step 1: Close on purchase of the house

Buyer (Builder) → Buys the house for $125,000 cash

Seller → Deposits $30,000 into a Certificate of Deposit at the local Bank

Bank → Makes a $125,000 loan to the Buyer (Builder)

Buyer (Builder) → Invests $0 cash investment in the purchase of the house

Step 2: Remodel and sell the house

Buyer (Builder) → Invests $30,000 in remodeling the house

Buyer (Builder) → Sells the remodeled house for a net sales price (after costs) of $180,000

Buyer (Builder) → Makes approximately a $25,000 net profit

Benefits

Benefit to the Seller (Older Couple):

The Sellers sold their house at full price.

The Sellers relieved themselves of the responsibility and the costs of a large house.

The Sellers earned interest on a portion of their sales proceeds by placing them in a Certificate of Deposit with a local bank, which they were going to do anyway.

Benefit to the Buyer:

The Buyer (Builder) completed a project and made a good profit upon the sale of the remodeled house.

The Buyer (Builder) also developed a business relationship with the locally based bank, which could be used for future projects in the neighborhood.

The Buyer (Builder) also developed the tool of compensating balances for other purchases.

Benefit to the Bank:

The Bank developed new business relations with both the Seller and the Buyer (Builder).

The Bank acquired some of the funds from the Certificate of Deposit to make the house loan to the Buyer (Builder).

CREATIVE DOWN PAYMENTS

COMMERCIAL OR INVESTMENT EXAMPLE

Dick Janson, a member of the Society of Exchange Counselors (SEC) in of Austin, Texas, had a national, credit-rated tenant who wanted a building built and leased to them under a Net-Net-Net" lease. A Net-Net-Net lease (sometimes described as a NNN lease) is one with all of the operating expenses paid by the tenant. These operating expenses include such items as property taxes, insurance and, maintenance.

This type of "Net-Net-Net" lease is in strong demand by potential Buyers. However, most of the typical buyers for this type of property want a completed building with a paying tenant occupying the building. The problem was that, while there would be buyers for the NNN leased property once the building was built and the lease started, Dick did not have the cash—about $700,000—to develop the property and build the building.

Normally, financing a Net-Net-Net leased building with a national tenant would be easy. However, the real estate development market in Austin was in a slump that mirrored a national economic slowdown. Banks already owned many commercial loans that were in default or in danger of going into default. Even on completed buildings, loans were not easy to obtain.

Furthermore, banks in the area were not interested in making a construction loan to build the building. There is more risk during the construction phase than at any other time during the total ownership period. That is because so many things can disrupt the construction schedule and budget. Bad weather, material shortages, builder fraud, labor strikes, changes in local politics, and an endless list of other potential problems all make a construction loan less desirable to a bank that a loan on a finished product.

One bank said they would normally have an interest, but a development loan at that time just represented too much risk for them.

SOLUTION

Dick asked the bank loan officer if they would make the loan if he could arrange a sizeable deposit into the bank. The loan officer agreed to consider that idea.

Dick asked an investor to put up $300,000 for a one-year Certificate of Deposit in the bank. Dick promised that the Certificate of Deposit would not be pledged to the bank for the loan in any way. The investor would receive a small amount of monthly interest from the bank as long as the money was invested in the Certificate of Deposit. As additional consideration for the investor purchasing the Certificate of Deposit at the bank, Dick's company also paid an additional return to the investor.

With this structure, the bank made the $700,000 construction loan. Even though the $300,000 Certificate of Deposit was not pledged as security for the loan, the money going into the lending bank reduced the risk of the loan in the banker's mind. In this case, safety was a matter of perception, not just some objective standard.

The Bank received 7 percent on the total $700,000 construction loan and paid out .5 percent on the $300,000 Certificate of Deposit. For the one-year term of the loan, they made a net interest profit of $47,500 with no additional net investment for that portion of the construction loan (see below). That $47,500 net interest profit represented an 11.88 percent yield on the net $400,000 loan by the bank. The calculation of the net yield to the bank is shown on the following chart:

CALCULATION OF NET YIELD TO BANK

Bank Loan to the Developer	$700,000
Bank Receives Deposit from the Investor	-$300,000
Total Interest Received by the Bank	
(7% Interest x $700,00 Bank Loan) =	$49,000
Less: Interest Paid by the Bank on the Certificate of Deposit (1/2% Interest x $300,000) =	-$1,500
Net Interest Received by the Bank	$47,500
Net Percentage Yield to the Bank	
($47,500 Net Interest / $400,000 Net Cash Investment) =	**11.88%** Yield

That 11.88 percent yield to the Bank on net cash invested by the Bank is substantially higher than the yield the bank would receive on a normal loan. It must be remembered, however, that the $300,000 invested in the Certificate of Deposit is not pledged for the $700,000 construction loan. The construction loans stands on this own in the event of any default by the Buyer / Developer.

Dick Janson built the building and the national tenant moved in under the long-term Net-Net-Net lease. Once the building was completed, Dick sold it for a good profit for himself and the investor.

SUMMARY OF TRANSACTION

Step 1: Buyer (Developer) writes contract to purchase land for development

Buyer (Developer) →Writes contract offering to purchase land

Buyer (Developer) → Includes contingency of obtaining financing to build a building on the site

Step 2: Buyer (Developer) negotiates the lease with credit-rated tenant

Buyer (Developer) → Includes contingency in lease of obtaining financing for the proposed development

Step 3: Buyer (Developer) → Finances the purchase of land and building costs

Investor → Deposits $300,000 into a Certificate of Deposit into the a Bank

Bank → Makes a $700,000 construction loan to the Buyer / Developer

Buyer (Developer) → Invests $0 cash in the land and building

Step 2: Buy land, build building, and sell

Buyer (Developer) → Buys the land and builds the building

Tenant → Moves into the building and starts paying on the Net-Net-Net lease

Buyer (Developer) → Receives monthly income from the Net-Net-Net lease

Buyer (Developer) → Sells the completed building for a profit

BENEFITS

Benefit to Developer (Dick Janson):

The Developer was able to build the building because he received the money from the loan.

The Bank made the loan partially because of the deposit of $300,000 for the Certificate of Deposit

The Developer received a 100 percent loan to cost. This is not typically available from a bank, even with a Net-Net-Net leased building with a national tenant.

The Developer made a profit from the lease income and from the sale of the leased building.

Benefit to the Investor:

The Investor received an excellent return from the combination of the Certificate of Deposit interest and the percentage of profits payments by the developer.

The Investor never risked any portion of the $300,000 invested in the Certificate of Deposit.

Benefit to the Bank:

The Bank made loan on the Net-Net-Net leased building with a national tenant. As a substantial kicker, they got a substantial amount of cash deposited in a one-year Certificate of Deposit. That deposit provided much of the initial funding for the loan and increased the Bank's yield on the construction loan.

KEY POINTS

Depositing money into the bank making a loan increases the yield to a bank by their lending out the amount of the deposit at a much higher interest rate. It also can make the loan safer in the mind of the representatives of the bank.

Sometimes the deposits made are in checking account balances with an agreement to leave the funds for a specific period of time and sometimes in a Certificate of Deposit with the same kind of agreement. There are also other financial instruments that a bank may consider as alternatives.

A bank might require that a loan be additionally secured by the deposits or they might not. This all depends on the situation of the real estate, the bank, and the borrower. It also depends upon the negotiation among all parties.

CONCLUSION

As you can see from these strategies presented, there are endless opportunities to use something other than cash as a down payment on real estate. Personal property, Certificates of Deposits or other financial instruments, other real estate, trade credits, and more are possible as down payments on real estate. The only limitations are your ability to understand these strategies and willingness to apply your own creativity and put these strategies into action.

As a buyer, you can offer something other than cash as a down payment. As a seller, you can look for motivated buyers who have something other than cash to purchase your property.

For example, you could:

- House as Down Payment

- Land as Down Payment

- Professional Services as a Down Payment

- Down Payment Equals Free and Clear Property

- Apply the Down Payment to the Monthly Debt Service

- Additional Collateral for Down Payment

- Borrow a Property as Collateral for Loan

- Deposit Money to Obtain a Loan

- Borrow a Certificate of Deposit to Obtain a Loan

CONCLUSION

You can access the most in each of these strategies by applying the "Fundamental Principles of Creative Real Estate":

Principle #1: Embrace Problems and Create Solutions

Principle #2: Get All of the Facts

Principle #3: Work with Motivated People

Principle #4: Create "Net Benefits" for Everyone Involved

Principle #5: It's About the People, Not Just the Property

Principle #6: Employ Qualified Professionals.

Using these "Fundamental Principles of Creative Real Estate" and the strategies we just summarized, will give you an enormous edge in closing real estate transactions.

And the more principles you use, the more likely your deals can—and often will—close.

Good offerings!

THANK YOU!

I hope you have enjoyed this second book in the *Creative Real Estate Book Series,* and you are equipped with more answers to close more real estate deals!

A FREE GIFT FOR READING THIS BOOK

Don't forget your *Free Creative Down Payment Checklist for* you to use in applying Creative Down Payments to everyday real estate transactions. Just go to *http://CreativeRealEstateNetwork/freegift2* and claim your free checklist.

And if you liked this book, you will love out our upcoming online Creative Real Estate courses on *http://CreativeRealEstateNetwork.com*!

RATE THIS BOOK

I invite to also go to my Amazon author page at http://ChuckSutherlandOnAmazon.com and rate and review this book. I would be very grateful and it will help others who are confused about how to creatively finance real estate get the answers they seek.

I would also appreciate it very much if you could leave a short book review on my Amazon author page located at *http://ChuckSutherlandOnAmazon.com* via the link below. It will help others like yourself decide if the *Creative Real Estate Book Series* is right for them.

Many thanks!

Chuck Sutherland

Chuck@CreativeRealEstateNetwork.com

GLOSSARY

Added Value - An amount added to the value of a product or service through entrepreneurship

Additional Collateral - Additional assets put up by a borrower as a second form of collateral to secure an obligation to repay a debt or perform some other action, sometimes required by the lender to reduce the risk of making a loan or to ensure that some other action is performed

All-Inclusive Deed of Trust - A Deed of Trust, which encompasses and includes all other Deeds of Trust that have a superior priority

All Inclusive Wrap-Around Mortgage - A Mortgage, which encompasses and includes all other mortgages that have a superior priority

Amortized - A loan with regular payments at an interval over a specific period of time, which completely pays off the principal and interest during that period

As Remodeled Value - The value of a property after repairs and improvements

Asking Price - The price at which a parcel of real estate is offered for sale

Assumption - Taking on another's responsibilities or financial obligation (such as a loan)

Balloon - Loan installment or other payment (paid usually at the end of the loan period) to substantially reduce or pay off a loan

Benefit - An advantage or profit gained from something

Boots on the Ground - Usually denotes a person who physically conducts or oversees the performance of some action

Capitalization Rate - The rate of return on a real estate investment property based on the expected income that the property (see Yield

Carrying Costs - The costs associated with owning a parcel of real estate

Closing - The completion of a transaction involving the sale or exchange or real estate

Closing Agent - An individual company that handles the closing of a parcel of real property and the legal transfer of title and ownership from the seller to the buyer

Collateral Security - Property pledged by a borrower to protect the interests of the lender

Consumer Credit - Credit extended to individuals for personal or household use, rather than to businesses

Conventional Financing - A loan that conforms to conditions and terms of the general financing marketplace. Sometimes refers to a loan other than one guaranteed by the Veterans Administration or insured by the Federal Housing Administration

Creative Financing - Financing that is outside the box of traditional real estate financing

Creditor - A person or entity to whom a debt is owed

Cross-collaterization - See Additional Collateral

Curb Appeal - The visual attractiveness of a property as viewed from the street

GLOSSARY

Deal - A financial transaction

Deed of Trust - In real estate, a deed of trust is a deed to real property that is transferred to a trustee that holds it as security for a loan (debt) between a borrower and lender

Detriment - A disadvantage or loss from something

Developer - A person or company that builds and sells houses or other buildings on a piece of land

Dodd-Frank Act - The Dodd-Frank Wall Street Reform and Consumer Protection Act, a compendium of federal regulations, primarily affecting financial institutions and their customers, Passed in 2010 and effective in January 2014

Down Payment - A part of the full purchase price paid at the time of purchase with the balance to come from the proceeds of a loan

Due Diligence - The process of investigating and researching a property or situation to determine actual or potential risks

Duplex - A two-unit property where the units are normally attached

Equity - The net value of a property after any debts and other obligations have been subtracted

Escrow - Money, deed, or some other asset held in trust by a third party to be turned over to the receiving party only upon fulfillment of one or more conditions

Escrow Account - A special account for holding specific monies for disbursement under specific conditions

Escrow Closing - The process of selling or buying a property where an independent third party holds and disburses all documents and money upon completion of the conditions of the closing.

Existing Financing - The current financing secured by a property and/or a guarantee

First Deed of Trust - A deed of trust first in priority before other deeds of trust

First Mortgage - A mortgage first in priority before other mortgages

Fix and Flip - To buy and usually renovate (real estate) so as to quickly resell at a higher price

Flip - To buy and usually resell property so as to quickly resell at a higher price

Free and Clear - Free from any debt or encumbrance

Guarantee - A promise for the fulfillment of something

Lease with a Contract to Purchase (Lease Purchase) - A lease of property for a specified time with an agreement to buy that property on or before a specified date

Lease with an Option to Purchase - A lease of property for a specified time with an option by the buyer to buy that property on or before a specified date

Loan Facilitator - An individual or company that manages the loan process in a closing of the purchase of property

Loan Security - The collateral assigned to a lender to secure the repayment of a loan

Loan to Value (LTV) - The amount of money borrowed in relation to the total market value of a property

Loan to Value Ratio (LTV%) The percentage calculated by dividing the total amount of the outstanding loans by the total value of the collateral.

Market Value - The most probable price that a property would bring in a competitive and open market under fair sale conditions

Market Value Appraisal - A professional opinion, usually written, of the market value of a property, such as a home, business, or other asset

Market Yield - The annual return of an investment divided by the market value

MLO - See Mortgage Loan Originator

Mortgage - A conveyance of or lien against property (as for securing a loan) that becomes void upon payment or performance according to stipulated terms

Mortgage Loan Originators (MLOs) - An individual or company that originates a mortgage in a real estate transaction

Mortgagee - The lender in a mortgage loan transaction

Mortgagor - The borrower in a mortgage loan transaction

Must-Have - In real estate, something that is essential to have or obtain by a party to the transaction

Nationwide Mortgage Licensing System & Registry (NMLS) - A national registry of mortgage loan originators (MLOs)

Net Benefits - The advantage or profit gained from something after consideration of the disadvantages and costs

Net-Net-Net Lease (NNN Lease) - A lease with all of the operating expenses paid by the tenant. These operating expenses include such items as property taxes, insurance, and maintenance

NNN Lease – See Net-Net-Net Lease

Net Operating Income (NOI) - The total of all sources of income, less vacancy, credit losses, and operating expenses

NMLA - See Nationwide Mortgage Licensing System & Registry

NOI - See Net Operating Income

Note - A written promise to pay a debt under specific terms and conditions

Opportunity Cost - The cost of using a resource to acquire one thing instead of another

Option - In real estate, a right to buy or sell something for a specified price during a specified period

Owner Value - The value that an owner of property places on that property

Ownership Costs - In real estate, the costs of owning a certain property, which include loan payments, taxes, maintenance, and management

Paper Lots - Lots located in a platted subdivision with no streets or utilities installed yet

Party or Parties - A person or entity that is involved in a legal case or contract

Percentage of Sale Proceeds – A calculated amount, typically for a loan payment, in order to obtain a partial release of collateral as security for a loan (for example, 40% x $100,000 sales proceeds equals a $40,000 loan payment)

Potential Market Value - The estimated price that a property would bring in a competitive and open market under fair sale conditions and under some assumptions as to how the property can be improved under a particular plan

Potential Net Operating Income - The estimated total of all sources of income, less vacancy, credit losses, and operating expenses under some assumptions as to how the property can be improved under a particular plan

Qualify (for a loan) - To meet the requirements or conditions to receive or assume a loan

REALTOR - A member of the National Association of Realtors

Recorded Mortgage - A legal instrument executed by the borrower and recorded of record assigning to the lender a legal claim on certain property as security for a loan

Release of Recorded Mortgage - A legal instrument executed by the lender and recorded of record proving the lender no longer has a legal claim on certain property as security for a loan

Relocation Company - A firm that arrange the relocation of the employees of a company or entity from one city to another

Remodeled Market Value - The estimated price that a property would bring in a competitive and open market under fair sale conditions and under some assumptions as to how the property can be remodeled under a particular plan

Remodeler - A person or company that remodels and improves real property

Remodeling Agreement - The agreement between the owner of a property and a person or company that remodels and improves real property

Return on Investment (ROI) - The results of an action compared to the costs. In real estate, the term refers to the percentage expressed by the financial yield divided by the cost of the investment

ROI - See Return on Investment

SAFE Act - The Secure and Fair Enforcement for Mortgage Licensing Act of 2008

Second Deed of Trust - A Deed of Trust second in priority behind another Deed of Trust

Second Mortgage - A Mortgage second in priority behind another Mortgage

Security - Something given as a pledge for the fulfillment of some obligation

Security Instrument – The document signed by the person or entity receiving a loan or making a promise and providing the collateral to ensure that the loan is repaid as agreed or the promise is kept, typically referring to the mortgage or trust deed that evidences the pledging of an asset or property as security

Seller Financing - The seller of a property making a loan for a buyer to purchase the seller's property

Subject To - Conditional or dependent on something

GLOSSARY

Subordinated - A debt or obligation that has a lower priority in repayment than some other debt or obligation

Sum-Certain - A specific dollar amount not subject to additional calculation

Sweat Equity - The value or results from the work that a person does to improve something

Third Deed of Trust - A Deed of Trust third in priority behind two other Deeds of Trust

Third Mortgage - A Mortgage third in priority behind two other Mortgages

Third-Party Lender - An independent lender not associated with the buyer or seller

Title Company - A company in the business of examining title to real estate and issuing title insurance, which often holds earnest money from a contract to sell real property and manages the closing process

Turn Around - The process of improving a poorly producing property through investment and management

Underwriting - The process during which lenders analyze the risks a particular borrower presents and either declines to make the loan or sets appropriate conditions for the loan

Underwriting Standards (or Requirements) - The minimum guidelines established by an investing, lending, or government regulatory entity to ensure that safe and secure investments or loans are made.

Value - The amount of money that something is worth

Wholesale Buyer - In real estate, an individual or company that buys property at a substantial discount below the estimated market value

Yield - The financial return of an investment, usually expressed as the net income divided by the amount of the total investment